Organic Gardening
in
Cold Climates

Sandra Perrin

Mountain Press Publishing Company
Missoula, Montana — 1991

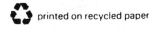 printed on recycled paper

Cover drawing by John Schneeberger

Library of Congress Cataloging-in-Publication Data

Perrin, Sandra.
    Organic gardening in cold climates / Sandra Perrin. — [Rev. and
expanded ed.]
        p.   cm.
    Rev. ed. of.: Organic gardening in Montana and the Northwest.
    Includes index.
    ISBN 0-87842-275-7 : $9.95
    1. Organic gardening—Snowbelt States. 2. Organic gardening—
Canada. I. Perrin, Sandra. Organic gardening in Montana and the
Northwest. II. Title.
SB453.5.P46   1991   ·   91-23308
635.0484'09795—dc20   CIP

Mountain Press Publishing Company
P.O. Box 2399
Missoula, Montana 59806
(406) 728-1900

To my father, who planted the seeds well and taught me to appreciate the simple and good things in life.

Table of Contents

Foreword

Anyone can garden with this book. It tells you exactly what you need to know. Even if you have never dug a spade into earth, this book will lead you step by step from bare ground—even ground that is now lawn—to a finished oasis of growing vegetables.

This is a book about organic gardening. What is organic gardening, you might ask. Does it work? Read on. Sandra Perrin is a happy, successful organic gardener in Missoula, Montana. She also believes in spreading the word. She teaches, lectures and writes. She has published articles in *Organic Gardening* magazine. This book is the result of years of experimenting with new varieties and new methods.

The section on varieties of vegetables that do well in the Northwest is invaluable. The short growing season makes every day count. You want red tomatoes instead of green ones; you want sweet corn that gives corn and not ten feet of stalk.

"Mulching" might be an unknown term to you now. "Sludge" might be another. How about "biological pest control"? "French intensive gardening"?

Sandra explains all these gardening terms in simple language. That is the marvel of this book. It is simple, easy to read, easy to follow.

But it does include the magic of gardening. Why are more people gardening than ever before? Partly, of course, to reap the harvest of low-cost, fresh-from-the-good-earth food.

But there is more. There is the relationship between the gardener and the earth. This is especially true of the organic gardener. You are in partnership with the soil. You treat the soil well and it will treat you well.

Follow Sandra's organic ways and you'll find yourself planting marigolds in the middle of your tomato patch, then leaning on your hoe and expounding to your neighbors on the virtues of companion planting. You'll be talking about a "year-round" garden and experimenting with greens in December and January.

You'll learn how to make compost, how to save seeds, how to help along "good" bugs while keeping the "bad" bugs in check.

Sandra says she wants this book to be a "simple explanation of good organic gardening."

Let it help you grow good food.

Kim Williams
Naturalist, teacher and author

Editors note: Kim Williams wrote this foreword in 1981 for the third edition of Sandra Perrin's Organic Gardening in Montana and the Northwest. *Sadly, she died in 1986. Although this current book is greatly revised and expanded upon, Kim Williams' message remains appropriate.*

Acknowledgements

I would like to thank my fellow gardeners who took the time to share their suggestions for this expanded and revised edition of my earlier book, *Organic Gardening in Montana and the Northwest.* Special thanks go to my husband, Ron, who typed the manuscript and learned a lot about gardening in the process.

I would also like to thank John Schneeberger for providing many of the illustrations, and credit the United States Department of Agriculture's *Gardening for Food and Fun* for theirs as well.

Permission to cite from *Western Fertilizer Handbook* has been granted by its publisher, Soil Improvement Committee, California Fertilizer Association.

Introduction

I was born in southern France and spent a good part of my childhood and teens on a small farm near Toulouse. My distractions were limited, but one of them was helping my father in the garden. We gardened organically, not by choice, but because it was the only method used at that time. Agricultural chemicals were not available and farms were still diverse. For example, our farm's manure had to be used for something—it made cheap fertilizer!

I grew up with good-tasting vegetables and lots of them. We sold the excess to city people who, during World War II, would bicycle the country roads looking for food to buy.

Later on I exchanged my country life for city life. But only when I came to Chicago in 1960 did I realize that I was missing something important. The tasteless vegetables I was buying made me yearn for the ones we grew in France.

It was time to garden again. My first one was in California in 1965, and I have planted every year since moving to Montana in 1969. It never entered my mind to use synthetic fertilizers or any other chemicals because I am too thrifty to do so. Instead, I use whatever organic materials I can put my hands on. It didn't take me long to realize that my organic garden grew well, with no pests, while my neighbors' were plagued with all sorts of infestations.

In gardening organically I follow a simple philosophy: I treat the soil well—as a living thing—and, in return, it becomes unconditionally generous. I have learned to be humbled at the sight of what a little seed and soil can do together. I also make sure, as a service to me, future generations, and planet Earth, that at the end of every season I leave my soil in as good or better condition than when I started.

Sandra Perrin. —photo by Nancy Erickson

Conventional gardening, on the other hand, concentrates on harvesting in quantity. Many conventional gardeners fertilize with chemicals designed to increase the year's yield, with little knowledge, concern, or respect for the soil. The future condition of the garden become less important than this year's yield.

While gardening in California offered me a wide range of crops I could grow easily, gardening in Montana posed a special challenge because of its cold climate. But the challenges posed by a short growing season did not deter me from gardening.

Gardening in a cold climate has made me more aware of my environment. I can't grow jicama or artichokes, but I can grow many other tasty vegetables, and my garden produces over a longer season than I or others expected.

I tuned in with the weather and looked around my yard, observing the growth patterns and finding natural microclimates that I put to use. I also created artificial microclimates with various season extenders.

Observation and ingenuity, together with vegetable varieties adapted to cold climates, have made my garden less limited. The end result is that I have taken the guesswork out of gardening in a cold climate. Vegetables grown organically taste better than store-bought produce. No store can offer lettuce with crackling leaves or tomatoes still warm from the sun. My vegetables have not been sprayed with pesticides or otherwise treated to enhance their cosmetic appearance or ease of shipment. I take great pride in providing my family and customers with healthy vegetables year-round from a backyard and front-yard garden.

I also cannot overlook the therapeutic value of growing a garden. Besides the physical exercise you get by working outside, you get what's good for the soul. Through the opportunity for family projects, the contribution an organic garden makes to a sound ecology, and the pleasure of watching a garden grow, you can relax, gain a better understanding of nature, gain a sense of accomplishment, and boost your self-esteem. None of these benefits can be measured in dollars, and it all happens in one growing season.

I have never become bored with gardening. Each year brings a new excitement, a new vegetable to grow, a new variety to try, a new problem to solve, and a new experience for my taste buds.

This book will guide you through the essentials of gardening in cold climates, emphasizing concise and practical advice for both novice and seasoned gardeners. The main virtue of this book is that it gathers under one cover, and in a simple form, the information you would collect only by reading many sources, and it eliminates the contradictions and confusion. I hope it will lead you to a successful and enjoyable garden.

CHAPTER 1

Planning Your Garden

Judging Soil Quality

Before you prepare your garden for planting, check your soil quality. Soil quality is based on texture, structure, and porosity. Texture refers to the size of soil particles. Structure denotes the size and properties of groups, or granules, of soil particles. The kind of granulation your soil has is important for you to know. It determines the type of cultivating and the amount of watering you will need to do. And, once you understand them, you can minimize problems caused by poor texture or structure by adding organic material to the soil.

Porosity refers to the size of the pore spaces between the soil granules. A clayish soil has small, tightly packed particles and, consequently, is difficult for water or roots to penetrate. A good soil is forty to sixty percent open space, which is filled with air or water.

Soils are grouped into four categories: clays, loams, sand, and gravel. Loam, a mixture of sand and clay, is the category of concern to gardeners. Loam varies in weight, and its structure can be changed with proper conditioning. For gardening, the ideal structure for loam is granular.

To determine the structure of your soil, dig out a square foot of your garden when it is not too wet. The ideal gardening soil should crumble between your fingers. If you find worms, take that as a good sign; it indicates that your soil is fertile and contains organic matter.

If you are a perfectionist, you can purchase a home-soil test kit to tell whether your soil has an adequate amount of the three major soil nutrients—nitrogen, phosphorus, and potassium. As an alternative contact your county extension agent, who will give you the information you need to have your soil analyzed professionally.

If your soil lacks any of the necessary nutrients you can bolster it organically. For a low-nitrogen soil, most organic gardeners add manure, but blood meal also works well. However, too much nitrogen can harm your plants. Because it enhances rapid growth, nitrogen promotes plant tissues that are watery, less nutritious, and more susceptible to disease. For example, excess nitrogen causes tomatoes to form abundant foliage and a poor crop of fruits.

You can counter a lack of phosphorus in your soil by adding manure, fish meal, bone meal (steamed or raw), and rock phosphate.

Be aware that bone meal will release phosphorous slowly into the soil, while rock phosphate, since it is water soluble, is more readily available to the plant and will act faster.

Finally, if your soil lacks potassium, steer, sheep, goat, or rabbit manure makes a good supplement. Other organic materials like granite dust, greensand, and wood ash are also high in potassium.

If your garden's soil doesn't measure up, don't give up gardening. Just start with a small plot, and build up the soil organically. You should see some improvement by the end of the first season, and next year your garden will look even better.

Testing Soil pH

In the old days gardeners tasted their soil to test its acidity. If it tasted sour or bitter, they knew it wasn't good for raising plants. But if it tasted sweet, they knew that they could expect high yields. Sour-tasting soil is too acid for most crops, and bitter soil is too alkaline for high yields. Tasting your soil is a primitive way of measuring the soil pH, but you do need to know what pH is and why it is important.

To measure certain soil characteristics the terms "acid," "neutral," and "alkaline" are used. A soil's pH indicate its acidity or alkalinity on a scale of 0 to 14. Thus, the middle of the pH scale is 7.00, or neutral. A soil pH below neutral is acidic and above neutral is alkaline. You need to know the pH of your garden soil because it releases its nutrients only when at a near-neutral pH. Nitrogen, phosphorous, and potassium are best available to plants at a soil pH between 6.5 and 7.5. A soil of this pH also offers the most favorable environment for large numbers of microorganisms, including bacteria that convert the nitrogen in the air to a form available to plants, and others that decompose plant tissue to form humus. Microorganisms, then, are vital to soil fertility. Strong acidic soil decreases total nutrient availability, and plants may literally starve to death.

If your soil is too acidic, you can modify it by adding agricultural limestone or wood ash. You can add either of these to compost, then mixing the finished compost with your soil.

Overly alkaline soils concentrate some salts until they become toxic to plants. You can modify these soils by adding sulphur or gypsum. Do not use wood ash or limestone in your compost if your soil is alkaline.

The cheapest way of finding your soil's pH is by using litmus paper, which you can find at some drugstores. After a rain, simply take a piece of litmus paper, and press it into the soil. If the test paper doesn't change color, other than darkening with moisture, your soil pH is about 7.0. If it turns blue, your soil is alkaline; if it turns pink it is acid. However, litmus paper will not tell you the degree of alkalinity or acidity in your soil. More sophisticated measurements are available for reasonable prices. They will give you accurate pH readings as well as indicating what soil supplements to use and how much of them is required.

Picking the Site

You can decide on the size of your garden by looking at four factors: How much space do you have available? How much time can you devote to it? How many people do you want it to support? What kind of vegetables do you want to grow in it?

A plot thirty feet by thirty feet is a reasonable size to feed four people, assuming you plant your rows much closer than indicated on the seed packets. With intensive gardening techniques, you can use significantly less space than with conventional gardening techniques to produce the same amount of food. (However, this will not hold true if you grow corn or potatoes.) (See *Intensive Gardening*, page 7.)

When you develop a new garden, particularly in a yard without much suitable space or sunlight, you can plant pocket gardens, dividing your vegetables into compatible groups and using small patches of available space wherever you find it.

Seed packets and catalogs tell you how long your rows will be if you plant your seeds with their recommended spacing. You will find this information useful when planning how much space to use for each variety. But remember, you can space your rows more closely than seed companies recommend.

If you have scant time for gardening, remember that thorough mulching can considerably reduce the amount of care, and time, your garden needs.

Two rules should be followed by all new gardeners picking a plot. First, a garden should have full exposure to the sun. Second, avoid cultivating spaces where nothing grows presently. Crab grass, in spite of the trouble it spells, indicates rich soil.

Finally, a fence is useful because it can be used for vines and offers some protection from wind, some animals, and light frosts.

Planning a Garden

Make the most of your space and your time. Careful planning will keep you from being overwhelmed by excessive amounts of food. Your garden should reflect the amount of time you will be able to spend with it. If you have a tight schedule, you should not overplant. Prepare a detailed plan for your garden before you order seeds or prepare the site. This will prevent wasted time and money.

Draw a rough sketch of your garden, using a scale of one-eighth inch per foot. Outline the shape of your garden, locate the rows, and plan for space between them. Determine how many row-feet you will devote to each vegetable, and where you will plant each one.

You can double your harvest by interplanting and succession planting. Interplanting takes full advantage of space available while crops are maturing. For instance, you can plant a row of radishes or spinach between rows of peas. The radishes or spinach will be ready to harvest before the peas are high enough to shade them. You can also interplant these crops between rows of carrots.

Succession planting involves replanting fast-growing vegetables (like radishes or spinach), or transplanting young plants that you have started indoors (like tomatoes or cucumbers), into areas where you

5

have harvested. In this way, you can use the space taken up by early harvested spring crops once more for later crops.

You can quadruple your garden's yield by using biodynamic intensive-gardening methods. (See **Biodynamic/French Intensive Raised Beds**, page 8.)

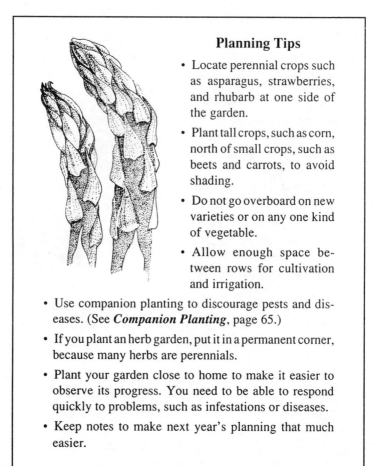

Planning Tips

- Locate perennial crops such as asparagus, strawberries, and rhubarb at one side of the garden.

- Plant tall crops, such as corn, north of small crops, such as beets and carrots, to avoid shading.

- Do not go overboard on new varieties or on any one kind of vegetable.

- Allow enough space between rows for cultivation and irrigation.

- Use companion planting to discourage pests and diseases. (See **Companion Planting**, page 65.)

- If you plant an herb garden, put it in a permanent corner, because many herbs are perennials.

- Plant your garden close to home to make it easier to observe its progress. You need to be able to respond quickly to problems, such as infestations or diseases.

- Keep notes to make next year's planning that much easier.

Intensive Gardening

The size of garden you need depends on the way you put your garden to work. If you have plenty of land to devote to a garden, you can be generous with your spacing; if you use a rototiller or a tractor, you will probably have to. However, it is unnecessary to have a huge garden, when you can reap as much food from a small one. A small backyard is no reason to forego a garden. And why not use the front yard as well? Vegetables are beautiful too!

Intensive gardening solves the small gardener's problem of space. Once you know how much space a vegetable needs to reach maturity, you leave only that much room when you plant or thin your seedlings. As the plants grow, they will touch each other and form a solid bed of vegetables. At this point you will discover two things:

1. The plants keep moisture in, and you have to water less often.
2. The plants choke out weeds, and you have to do less cultivation or weeding.

If you decide to use the intensive method, fertilize your soil well, since you will have a higher concentration of plants to feed. And, when you use the intensive method, you need to make paths for yourself; you may prefer making raised beds.

Raised Beds

You have several techniques to choose from for making raised beds.

Simple Bed: After you have prepared your soil for planting you have to decide how long and wide to make your beds. You can make the beds as long as you want, but don't make them more than five feet wide. You should be able to reach the middle of the bed from both sides without straining your back. If you're planting vegetables that will need staking, such as many of tomato varieties, make the bed narrower.

Mark the pattern of your bed with a string. With a shovel make a path about eight inches deep and one foot wide with the string in the middle. Follow the string, and throw the dirt equally on both sides of the path. When you have dug around the string you will have created a bed. With a rake you can smooth the top flat and give it slanted edges, or you can rake it into a long mound. Remember that if you have marked your bed to be five feet wide, you will end up with four feet of planting space because of the path.

Biodynamic/French Intensive Raised Beds: Biodynamic/French Intensive is a long name for a relatively simple method that combines old Chinese, Greek, and French methods with modern science. It takes a comprehensive approach to organic gardening. For example, biodynamic regards composting as more than a proper carbon-nitrogen ratio. Biodynamic compost is custom-designed to achieve a microbial balance that will enhance a specific soil or solve a specific gardening problem. The preparation of a biodynamic bed requires the special effort of double digging. For this you will need a square spade and a garden fork—both preferably with D handles—plus a rake and a wheelbarrow.

To double dig, first mark out your bed. A five-foot wide bed is typical, but design your bed to fit your plants and your body.

Place the wheelbarrow at either end of the bed, where you will start your work. With your spade, dig a strip about ten inches wide and one foot deep across the bed. (If your trench averages less than a foot deep, that's all right.) Put every bit of that soil in the wheelbarrow. The square spade will allow you to dig straight down, which is difficult to do with a rounded shovel.

When you've finished the trench, use the fork to loosen the soil and subsoil exposed at the bottom of the trench. Remove any large rocks. You should be able to work the subsoil to a depth of about eight inches with the fork.

Next, with your spade, dig another trench parallel to the trench you just completed. Push forward each spadeful of soil from the new trench into the old trench. Thus, you don't turn the soil under but instead keep the nutrient-rich topsoil close to the root system of the plants. With the fork, loosen the soil at the bottom of the new trench. This allows the plants' roots to go deeper in search of extra nutrients. Repeat the sequence until you reach the end of your bed. Fill the last, empty bed with the soil from the wheelbarrow. You are now finished double digging

Shape the bed with a rake. You want to mound your soil from eight to twelve inches high. You can expect a higher mound if your soil is clayish. As you shape the bed, build a lip on all sides so that water won't erode the soil.

Finally, spread manure, compost, bone meal, or other soil amendments over the surface of the bed. Work them into the top six inches of your soil with the fork.

You will find it takes six to ten hours to build and plant a five by twenty foot biodynamic raised bed. Start with one bed, and use it for a season so you can see how well it works for you. Then build the next one.

Contained Raised Beds: For this version, prepare your soil any way you wish and contain it within the frame of your choice. Old logs are ideal. These beds are neat and permanent.

Raised beds and intensive gardening offer many advantages.

1. You never step on your plants.
2. You eliminate cultivation, because the soil stays loose.
3. You eliminate most weeding, because the closely spaced plants choke out the weeds.
4. You decrease watering, because the plants mulch themselves.
5. You can expect up to four times as many vegetables than from a conventional garden with the same space.

Intensive gardening, biodynamic bed-building, and every other gardening technique will seriously insult your imagination if you follow every step blindly. Every gardener should experiment and adapt. Create your own version of a raised bed.

Selecting Tools

Invest in good quality tools. They last longer, stay sharp, perform better, and, in the long run, save you money.

Shovel

You will find a shovel with a D or long handle handy for turning the soil, making holes when transplanting, moving dirt or manure, and making paths.

Hoe

A hoe is a multipurpose tool used to decapitate weeds, and to cultivate and mound the soil. You can use it to make wide or narrow furrows at planting time. Work a standard hoe at an angle for narrow furrows and flat for wide ones. You will also find hoes designed in a variety of styles to fit special needs.

Rake

The rake is essential for removing stones and roots, breaking up lumps of soil, leveling, and smoothing the surface of the soil before planting. In the fall you will find the rake useful for collecting debris. (Remember! If you have to interrupt your work, leave your rake with the working side down. This will prevent unnecessarily lost teeth and bruised noses.)

Trowel

A trowel is handy to transplant small plants or to uproot nasty weeds. Buy a good trowel, since inexpensive ones tend to bend and break at the shoulder when used in heavy soil.

Hand Cultivator

A hand cultivator, with a long handle for a large garden or with a short handle for small tracts, is well worth your investment. You can use a cultivator to aerate and weed the soil around your plants. It is a tool to grab when you want to converse with your plants, enabling you to dislodge a weed here or stir the soil there. Your cultivator will become an extension of your arm.

Wheelbarrow or Cart

A wheelbarrow or a cart is optional but nice. If you need to choose between the two, the cart will be easier on your back.

Rototiller

Do you need a rototiller? If your garden is small (less than 2,000 square feet), you'll find the investment difficult to justify. For a small rental fee you can have your garden rototilled, without worrying about the upkeep and storage of an expensive piece of equipment.

If you decide to double-dig for intensive raised beds you will need two additional tools: a garden spade and a spading fork.

Garden Spade

The spade, with its square blade, is for digging but you will also find it useful for making straight edging in your garden.

Spading Fork

The fork is a versatile tool. You can use it instead of a shovel to turn the soil, to aerate the subsoil, and to loosen up the soil before pulling out long-rooted vegetables. Wherever your soil has been compacted you'll find a spading fork invaluable.

* * *

When you put your tools to bed for the winter, clean them, apply some oil to prevent them from rusting, and keep them together in one place.

CHAPTER 2

Preparing Your Soil

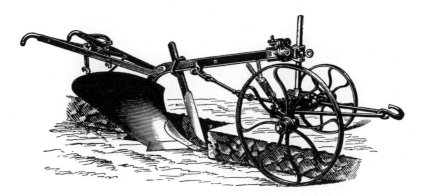

Preparing an Established Garden

To prepare the soil of an established garden first spread manure or finished compost on its surface. Spread cow or horse manure about one inch deep. However, you can't add too much compost; put it on as thick as you want.

Till the soil to a depth of six to eight inches. You don't need to rototill; spading turns the soil as well as a rototiller and leaves your earthworms intact.

Aristotle called earthworms the intestines of the soil. They actually produce topsoil by breaking down organic matter and burrowing deep into the subsoil, then bringing nutrients up to your plants. Earthworms neutralize both acid and alkaline soil, and, after they die, their decaying bodies provide excellent fertilizer. Of all the creatures important to the gardener, none is more important than the earthworm. Earthworms feed only on organic matter, so the more organic matter you add to the soil, the more worms you will have.

After tilling, go over the ground several times with a steel rake. Work the soil until it's smooth and loose, without any lumps.

Breaking Virgin Ground

You can turn any backyard, front yard, or vacant lot into a successful garden—even relatively late in the gardening season.

Look for an area that receives plenty of sunshine and check the soil: How deep is it? How compacted is it? What sort of material does it contain? Take a shovel and dig one-foot square holes at two or three different places in your plot. Notice the condition of your soil: Is it deep, shallow, clayish, sandy, soggy, dry? (See *Judging Soil Quality*, page 2.)

Turning a Lawn into a Garden

Option I

This option assumes that after you remove the sod, you have more than four inches of soil.

When you replace a lawn with garden you can rent a special tool to peel off the sod. Don't discard the sod. Keep it as a foundation for a compost pile, or let it sit in a corner—by next year it will turn into good soil. If your plot is short of topsoil, shake the sod, and scrape it over the teeth of a rake to save more soil.

After removing the sod, spread manure and compost, and spade or rototill the plot. Once raked, the soil is ready for planting.

Option II

Many modern lawns are built on a skimpy four inches of soil. Even with the sod on you have little soil to turn; if you use a rototiller you will surely damage the blades.

In this case spread three to four inches of good soil over the lawn area you have designated to become garden. Spread manure or compost if necessary, rake and plant. This method brings surprisingly good results the first year with short-rooted vegetables such as lettuces and other greens. The following season you can count on an even better garden.

Option III

In this case, you rototill the lawn without peeling off the sod. After rototilling you will have to rake out the lumpy roots. This is tedious, and it does not eliminate all the roots; whatever is left will interfere with your vegetables, especially the root crops. Moreover, if you have quack grass, the roots will be cut into a million pieces, with each one capable of sprouting into a new pest. However, if you have a relatively weed-free lawn, the pieces of sod left in your garden will turn into organic matter by the end of the season.

Option IV

This carefree approach is ideal for the gardener who can plan ahead.
Cover your lawn with black plastic film, an old rug, flattened cardboard, or anything that will blanket the garden area. You must do this at least six weeks before tilling. While covered, the plants will die and decompose at a rate depending on how warm the weather is.

Option V

You have peeled the sod or killed the grass; you have a thin layer of soil; and you can't, or don't want to, bring in new soil. You still can have a garden! Make beds! (See *Simple Bed*, page 7.) Beds automatically increase the depth of your soil, and by selecting short-rooted vegetable varieties you can have a decent garden. (For example, plant varieties of carrots such as Short'n Sweet and Little Finger, available from Burpee, or a round variety like Planet, available from Stokes.)

15

Shortcuts for Preparing a First-time Garden

- Place seed potatoes on your lawn and cover them with six inches of leaf mold or other suitable mulch. Your grass will die, and your potatoes will grow.

- For plants in the cabbage family (or for tomatoes, peppers, or eggplants), dig a small hole in the lawn, mix bone meal, manure or compost with the soil, and refill the hole. Cover the area with black plastic. Slash the plastic over the holes and plant the seedlings.

- In late August cover your lawn with four inches of straw or a similar material. The hot weather will quickly kill the grass. After a week or two cover the straw with compost or manure. When spring rolls around, you'll have powerful soil.

- Since you don't plant your entire garden at the same time, prepare only one bed at a time as the planting season unfolds and you need more space.

Organic vs. Chemical Fertilizers

Farmers grow most crops in the United States using massive amounts of chemical fertilizer and poisonous sprays. Researchers have documented well the harmful effects of sprays, but the value of chemical fertilizers causes more controversy.

On the one hand, many knowledgeable horticulturalists recommend chemical fertilizers, and, in the face of worldwide starvation, farmers around the world clamor for all they can get. Chemical fertilizers have caused phenomenal increases in yields since the German chemist Justus von Liebig discovered them more than 130 years ago. Also, considerable evidence demonstrates that organic fertilizers—the alternative to chemicals—must break down to inorganic form before plants can use them, thus making organic fertilizers less effective in the short run.

On the other hand, another school of thought condemns all chemical fertilizer as destructive to both soil and human health. These people contend that in the process of providing plants with large quantities of nutrients chemical fertilizers drastically weaken the plant-soil digestive system, eventually reducing the soil to a sterile medium.

Chemical fertilizers require for their production a significant part of the wasteful amount of energy the United States expends on food production. In this country we burn five calories of energy, on the average, to produce each calorie of food. This ratio does not take into account the energy required to manufacture farm machinery or to store and distribute food. If we begin to use organic methods on a grand scale, we can cut this huge energy drain by allowing earthworms and soil bacteria to do the work that chemicals now do to predigest fertilizer for the soil.

Feeding plants chemically is just like feeding people intravenously. Chemical farming bypasses the soil's digestive capabilities and feeds the plant directly. If growers add only chemicals the soil gradually loses its natural ability to digest nutrients. Plants grown on this sort of soil become reliant on a chemical diet.

In contrast, organic techniques can preserve and restore the world's limited reserves of topsoil. Since the beginning of this century modern agricultural techniques have caused the loss of up to sixty percent of our prime farming soil. Since it takes 200 to 500 years for an inch of topsoil to form, this has created an alarming situation in the United States. In view of a growing population's future food needs, the deterioration of our soil base has forced the U. S. Department of Agriculture to take a second, more favorable, look at the organic approach.

Manure and Other Fertilizers

Compost makes the best organic fertilizer and soil conditioner, but when it's not available, manure makes a fine substitute. How to apply manure properly confuses many gardeners, because, depending on the type of animal it comes from, the composition of manure varies. Dry and fresh manures also differ. Dry or well-rotted manure weighs less and loses volume more rapidly than fresh.

You can use fresh manure without harming your plants when you apply it properly, but well-rotted manure—manure at least a year old—is certainly preferable.

If you can get manure from a farm, take it from a pile rather than the floor of the barnyard since piled manure rots much more quickly and holds its fertility longer. For a garden of 300 square feet, one

cubic yard of well-rotted manure will cover the surface with about one inch. (A loaded pickup carries two cubic yards.)

Cows and horses supply the most commonly used manure. Sheep, rabbit, and poultry manure is much more potent, so use it sparingly—no more than fifteen pounds dry weight for each fifty square feet of soil.

Other organic fertilizers include bone meal, fish meal, blood meal, and sludge. You can buy these fertilizers from nurseries or garden supply stores. Most retailers sell them in prepackaged form with analyses and instructions that help to simplify their application for gardeners. Compared to manure you use small quantities of these fertilizers, with each one having a well-defined use.

Fertilizer analyses always list the three main nutrients indispensable to normal plant growth. The manufacturer indicates the fertilizer's nutrient content with letters and numbers: N (nitrogen), P (phosphorus) and K (potassium). For example, if you have a label bearing the numbers 10-5-3 you have a fertilizer containing 10 percent nitrogen, 5 percent phosphorus and 3 percent potassium.

Plants need nitrogen for above-ground growth. It ensures that plants grow quickly and have beautiful green foliage. Nitrogen helps plants form proteins and other compounds, such as chlorophyll.

Phosphorus is indispensable for the early and healthy development of plants, including root formation. In cold weather phosphorus is the nutrient that ensures good root and leaf growth.

Potassium is also essential for healthy root development, as well as helping plants protect themselves from disease. With the help of potassium plants produce carbohydrates and proteins. In root crops like potatoes, potassium ensures a good formation of starch.

In addition to nitrogen, phosphorus, and potassium plants need small amounts of other nutrients called trace elements. Some analyses list them, with the most commonly mentioned being calcium, copper, zinc, and manganese. Healthy soil usually provides trace elements, and rarely will specific problems during a plant's development make it necessary to add them.

Average Analysis of Organic Material

	Nitrogen % N	Phosphoric Acid % P_2O_5	Potasium Oxide % K_2O	Organic Matter % O.M.	Cubic Feet per Ton
Bulky organic materials					
Goat manure	2.77	1.78	2.88	60	70
Dairy manure	0.7	0.30	0.65	30	55
Steer manure	2.0	0.54	1.92	60	70
Horse manure	0.7	0.34	0.52	60	75
Hog manure	1.0	0.75	0.85	30	60
Sheep manure	2.0	1.00	2.50	60	70
Rabbit manure	2.0	1.33	1.20	50	70
Poultry manure	1.6	1.25	1.9	50	50
Seaweed (kelp)	0.2	0.1	0.6	80	—
Alfalfa hay	2.5	0.50	2.10	85	—
Alfalfa straw	1.5	0.30	1.50	82	—
Bean straw	1.2	0.25	1.25	82	—
Grain straw	0.6	0.20	1.10	80	—
Cotton gin trash	0.7	0.18	1.19	80	—
Winery pomace (dried)	1 to 2.0	1.5	0.5 to 1.0	80	—
Olive pomace	1.2	0.8	0.5	80	—
Organic Concentrate					
Dried blood	13.0	1.5	—	80	—
Fish meal	10.4	5.9	—	80	—
Digested sewage sludge	2.0	3.01	—	50	—
Activated sewage sludge	6.5	3.4	—	0.3	—
Tankage	7.0	8.6	1.5	80	—
Cottonseed meal	6.5	3.0	1.5	80	—
Bat guano	13.0	5.0	2.0	30	—
Bone meal*	*	*	—	—	—
Castor pomace	6.0	2.5-3.0	0.5	80	—

*There is a wide variation in the average percentages found in bone meal. Average found in analysis of 22 samples ran as follows.

Steamed Bone Meal

Nitrogen, %	Available Phosphoric Acid, %	Insoluble Phosphoric Acid, %	Total Phosphoric Acid, %
less than 1.00	12-14	14.16	12 - 14

All organic material should be purchased on the basis of actual analysis. There is a wide variation in value due to moisture content, type of storage and other conditions. These values are only averages taken from official literature.

Sludge deserves a special note. Some communities treat their sewage waste, turning it into sludge, a fertilizer with good qualities. However, since each community's waste has different components, before you use sludge you should learn about the treatment process, and, above all, whether you can safely use the finished product in your vegetable garden.

Compost

A compost pile is a small intensified version of nature's soil-building process. Unfortunately, poorly constructed compost piles

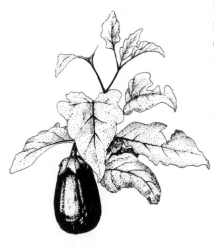

lead to rot and smell rather than fertilizer, occasionally causing distress to your neighbors. However, a well-constructed compost pile encourages a high rate of activity among bacteria and cooks the smell out of manure and kitchen wastes.

What is compost? It results from the decomposition of different organic materials. It has a blackish color and crumbs easily. When it fully decomposes, it becomes humus. Compost is both a complete organic fertilizer and an ideal soil conditioner.

Two types of bacteria can actively compost organic materials: aerobic (with oxygen) and anaerobic (without oxygen).

Aerobic Composting

Most gardeners prefer to compost their organic wastes aerobically. Crucial to this process are bacteria and fungi that need oxygen. To live, grow and multiply, these microorganisms need food, which they get from the nitrogen contained in organic materials. When the microorganisms die, their bodies' nutrients become available to the plants in a soluble chemical form. These soluble nutrients are lodged in the humus, which acts as a chemical clearinghouse. Due to the structure of humus, the nutrients do not leach out but are released to the plants over a long period.

Preparing compost is easy and inexpensive because you can use materials that come from every corner of your land and household—leaves, grass clippings, food wastes (except fats and meat), weeds, and manure from cows, goats, sheep, or rabbits.

Compostable materials fall into two categories: carbon (C) and nitrogen (N). The term "carbon/nitrogen ratio" (C/N) refers to the proper balance of compost ingredients high in carbon (straw, hay, dry leaves, etc.) and wet compost ingredients high in nitrogen (grass clippings, kitchen refuse, manure, etc.).

Each material used in your compost pile has its own, differing, C/N ratio and there is no simple way of determining the C/N content of each ingredient. But you should not worry about this. By layering your compost pile with equal amounts of dry material high in carbon and wet or green materials high in nitrogen, you will obtain a satisfactory ratio. Since nitrogen feeds the bacteria, making the process of composting possible, and manure is high in nitrogen, periodic sprinklings of manure will help to accelerate the composting process.

Many formulas have been developed for constructing a compost pile. Here is a simple but effective one for the home gardener:

To start, build a simple frame out of scrap lumber and chicken wire or screen material. Make sure the screening is two-inch mesh or less—tight enough to prevent the materials from falling out. The frame contains the compost pile and protects it from animals. A good size frame for the home gardener is one three feet high by three to four feet across. You can build your frame square, rectangular or circular; shape does not matter. For better aeration you can place a tube of wire netting in the center of the pile before adding any material. (With ingenuity you can build your own contraption. For example, in some communities you can obtain wooden pallets for free, and by attaching hinges you can make a good-looking bin in a jiffy. Pallets also have the advantage of allowing for good aeration.)

Now you're ready to feed the compost pile. Spread a six-inch layer of plant wastes on the bottom of the compost frame. Add a two-inch

layer of manure, and over this layer topsoil one-eighth to a quarter inch thick. Then add a sprinkling of lime, rock phosphate, granite dust, or wood ash to increase the mineral content of the compost and prevent it from becoming too acidic. (Don't feel guilty about skipping this step; these materials are not essential.) Water the pile and continue the process of layering, trying to balance dry (carbon) and wet (nitrogen) ingredients.

Within a few days the pile will begin heating up, which means that the microorganisms are at work. You can expect the temperature in the center of the pile to go as high as 160 degrees. With this kind of heat, you know that the weeds and diseases are being cooked out. However, if you are unsure of your composting skills, it is better not to compost diseased plants.

After two or three weeks the pile begins to shrink, which means it is time to turn it with a pitchfork. Turn it again about five weeks later. Regular turning feeds oxygen to your microorganisms. While turning the compost be careful to transfer the outer portion of the pile to the center so it can decay fully. Be sure your pile is not too wide if you want to turn it without breaking your back! In the summer your compost will be finished in about three months. It will take longer if you start the process in the fall.

You might wonder if commercial compost starters (bacteria in a dormant state) or commercial activators (chemical fertilizers) will improve the quality of your compost. You will be happy to know that the soil you add to your compost pile is full of the necessary bacteria, and by adding manure you provide those bacteria with all the additional nitrogen they need.

Problems
Compost does not heat up: Watering the pile might solve the problem. **Smelly pile:** An ammonia smell indicates that a different set of bacteria has gone to work; the anaerobic ones have replaced the aerobic ones. In this case too much moisture has smothered the aerobic microorganisms. You can solve the problem by turning the pile and adding more dry materials.

Anaerobic Composting

Even though anaerobic composting is not a popular method—because of its strong smell and slow decaying process—it does have advantages. The main one is that you do not have to turn the pile. Moreover, you can avoid objectionable smells by covering the pile with a layer of dirt, straw, or black plastic.

Another advantage is that anaerobic composting is well suited to the small garden with limited organic materials. A simple method for anaerobic composting is to fit a garbage can, of any size, with a plastic bag. Then fill it with layers of organic material. When the can is full, water the mixture (but only if it is dry), tie the bag, and place the cover on the garbage can. If you want the material to compost faster, place your full plastic bag where it is exposed to the sun, making sure animals cannot get to it (for example, on an accessible low roof).

Lazy Composting

Not everyone is enthusiastic about turning a compost pile. But don't worry, you can compost directly in your garden by using the trench composting method.

If you choose this approach, arm yourself with a shovel, make a small hole in a selected area of your garden, place your organic refuse in the hole and cover it with the soil you have just removed. This system is incredibly efficient. If done in the summer, total decay occurs within the growing season; if done in the fall, the compost will be ready by the next spring. If you want to be well organized about this method, you can allocate a whole row to trenching. When you finish the first row, start a second row next to the first. Depending on the size of your trenches and how quickly you collect compostable materials, by the time you start filling the third row, the first one will be ready for planting.

* * *

You commonly see gardeners dumping weeds in a bucket then stuffing them into a plastic bag for the garbage collectors to pick up. This procedure is wasteful. You can usually find an inconspicuous corner of your garden or yard where you can pile up the weeds and cover them with black plastic. By the following season you will have rich soil you can add to your garden. Approach your soil as if it were gold—do not throw it away!

CHAPTER 3

Planting in Cold Climates

Starting Plants Indoors

For a cold-climate gardener, spring fever means planting the seeds of those vegetables that need a head start if you want to see their fruit before the frost comes next fall. You can grow seedlings successfully indoors with some pampering.

An advantage to starting your own seedlings is that you can experiment with varieties unavailable at the local nursery.

The most popular vegetables started indoors are peppers, tomatoes, eggplants, broccoli, cauliflower, Brussels sprouts, cabbages, and head lettuce. (See *Varieties for Cold Climates*, page 83, to pick the variety best suited for you.)

Since germination periods and growth rates vary, you'll have to start your indoor vegetables at different times.

Peppers: Start ten to twelve weeks before you expect the last spring frost. Tomatoes: Start eight weeks before planting time. Eggplants: Plant eight to ten weeks before last frost.

You can plant broccoli, Brussels sprouts, cabbage, cauliflower, and head lettuce four to six weeks before last frost, and, since they can withstand light frost, they can go into the ground before the pepper and tomato plants. You can sow frost-hardy vegetables directly in the garden, but you will have to add one month to their maturation times. By using both techniques—indoor and outdoor planting—you can stagger your crops.

Planted indoors, cole family seeds require special attention. Unlike eggplants and pepper seeds, which are tender seeds and need a relatively high temperature to germinate (76-80 degrees F.), the cabbage family and lettuce seeds belong to the hard seed category and will germinate properly only in cool temperatures (50-60 degrees F.). That's why cabbage and lettuce seedlings can be grown on window sills, where temperatures are considerably cooler than you might expect—particularly at night. As a matter of fact, legginess in cole plants can come from it being too warm in your house.

You can start corn four to eight weeks before the last frost date: it transplants reasonably well. You can start squash, cucumbers, and melons four to five weeks before the last frost date, but these crops demand delicate handling. They despise having their root systems disturbed. Plant their seeds in individual containers from the beginning, preferably the same ones that you will set in the garden. You might discover that when you plant squash, cucumber and melon seeds outside, directly into warm soil, the plants will catch up with transplanted seedlings.

Soil for Seedlings

Pampering your indoor plants begins with preparing a good starting medium for the seeds. The classic mixture combines equal parts of garden loam, sand, and compost (or peat moss).

The most common problem you may encounter when starting seedlings is that they topple over and die shortly after they have appeared. This disease is called damping-off and is caused by fungi present in the soil.

To avoid damping-off you can do several things:

- Pasteurize your soil before planting seeds in it by baking it in your oven for an hour at 180 degrees F.. Place the soil in an oven baking bag to avoid odors in your house.

- Plant your seeds sparsely.

- Maintain a temperature of 60-70 degrees F. during germination (unless your seeds require a higher temperature to germinate, like peppers).

- Keep your soil damp but not soggy.

The porosity of your starting medium is another important factor in keeping your seedlings healthy. A light starting soil helps seedlings quickly develop vigorous root systems. Besides, a light medium makes it much easier to transplant your seedlings without damaging their roots. Mix sand or vermiculite (available at garden supply stores) with your soil to lighten it.

After you have mixed the starting medium, you have to moisten it. You can simply put the mixture in a plastic bag, add water, mix and close the bag for a couple of hours; by that time the water will be absorbed and you can add more, if necessary. Be conservative with water at first. To test the mixture for the right degree of dampness, take some in your palm and press it into a ball. When you open your hand the ball should crumble.

27

If you do not trust your own soil, you can use store-bought planting mixes. You will find many types of starting media readily available, but most are too heavy for your seedlings. To lighten them add some vermiculite.

You can start plants in a sterile medium like vermiculite. The seeds contain enough nourishment to sustain the seedling until the the first true leaves form. To keep the seedlings in a sterile medium for a longer time before transplanting into individual containers, you will have to fertilize them once a week. Use a mixture of two tablespoons of fish emulsion to a gallon of water (or use another fertilizer). Use the fish emulsion mixture once a week to fertilize any transplants.

You can also start your seeds using peat pellets (such as Jiffy-7). These dollar-shaped pellets are made of highly compressed peat moss mixed with plant nutrients, and enclosed in a plastic net. When soaked in water they quickly swell into a cylinder about one and three quarters inches in diameter by two and a quarter inches in height. You can sow seeds directly in them or use them for transplants. The pellets support seedlings until it is time for the plants to go out in the garden. Peat pellets are expensive, but if you do not grow too many plants, you'll find the investment worthwhile.

Planting Indoors

You can make cheap containers for starting seeds out of half-gallon milk cartons cut lengthwise into two pieces, three inches high. Margarine and cottage cheese containers, paper cups, etc., also work well. Wash the containers with hot water and soap. Make holes in the bottoms to ensure drainage, and fill your cartons with the moistened soil mixture. Press it down until the mixture feels resilient. You are now ready to put in your seeds.

Nurseries sell convenient plastic seedling trays. If you end up with this type of tray after buying plants, do not throw them away. Trays have advantages: you can plant your seeds in rows and one tray can host many seedlings. You have to make sure to plant only one kind of vegetable per tray. In addition, if you plant more than one variety of a single vegetable, it is imperative to use reliable identification—a permanent marker or tape that will stay put. Nothing is more disconcerting than mixed-up varieties.

Here are three methods of planting:

Method One: Put your seeds on top of the starting mixture, press them down gently and cover them lightly with some of the starting medium. Use a covering of a quarter inch for larger seeds like peppers and tomatoes and less for smaller seeds. For very small seeds, like celery, just press them into the soil, and do not cover.

Method Two: Place a half inch of milled sphagnum (or peat) moss on the bottom of the container. Fill the rest of the container with potting soil. Plant the seeds, cover with another quarter inch of sphagnum moss, and pat down. For cole crops, press the seeds into the soil without using the moss as a covering.

You can also add sphagnum moss to your potting soil to lighten the mixture.

Method Three: Use moistened vermiculite instead of potting soil. Vermiculite is a sterile medium and will eliminate the problem of damping-off. Lightly water the vermiculite with tepid water. Plant the seeds and cover them lightly with the same medium. Be sure to transplant the seedlings after they show their first true leaves.

Germination and Lighting

Place your seeded containers in plastic bags, making miniature greenhouses, and then tuck them in a warm, dark place. Germination periods vary between kinds of seeds.

Peppers germinate in about ten days at a temperature of 70 to 80 degrees F. Tomatoes germinate in five to eight days, when kept at 65 to 70 degrees F. Eggplants will germinate in eight to fourteen days. Unlike eggplants and peppers, which have tender seeds and require a relatively high temperature to germinate, cole crops and lettuce have hard seeds that require cool temperatures (50 to 60 degrees F.) to germinate.

Your seedlings need special treatment when they first appear so they don't develop long, spindly stems, that is, become "leggy." When the seedlings just emerge from the soil, remove the plastic bags and expose them to the light. To mature into healthy plants, the seedlings need to be exposed to good light, as close as possible to the spectrum of sunshine. A window sill located on the south or southwest will give adequate light if the sun is shining; however, winter days are still short and often cloudy. As a consequence, plants will become leggy and weak. Even though you think the light around you is adequate, it is not necessarily adequate for the growing plant.

But even without sunlight you can successfully grow plants by using artificial lights. And you don't have to reproduce the entire spectrum of sunshine. Fluorescent lights can substitute for natural light when it is not available. Mostly blue in their spectrum, fluorescents give out a light that will not overheat the plants, a cool light well suited for seedlings. You can buy fluorescent lights as a two-tube fixture with a white reflector and chains that will help you raise or lower it according to your plants' needs. For seedlings, 48-inch, 40-watt tubes are best; a 30-inch tube is less effective since the ends project poor light. Even if you buy a 48-inch tube remember that the best lighting will be in the middle. This type of fixture will give adequate light for a space 48 by 12 inches. The strength of a fluorescent light will decrease with age, and you should therefore change the tubes every 8,000 hours.

When seedlings first emerge you can give them continuous lighting during the first two weeks. At that point they need some rest and should get fourteen to sixteen hours of light per day. Place the light three to four inches above the plants, and as they grow hoist the fixture higher. Be sure leaves do not touch the bulbs.

Be aware that although the seeds of warm and cool season vegetables germinate better at warm temperatures, seedlings prefer to grow at cooler temperatures. Warm season seedlings prefer nights in the 60s and days in the 70s while the cool season seedlings will like nights in the 45 to 50 degree range. Included in the cool-season category are tomato plants. They will produce better crops if grown with lower night temperatures.

Watering and Thinning

Seedlings are fragile and need careful watering. It is easy to overwater them—they don't like wet feet. A small watering can with a long spout is a practical tool for this job. Use tepid or room-temperature water instead of cold tap water for your seedlings. When you see water coming out of the bottom of the container, stop watering. How often you need to water depends on the medium and how many seedlings you have in your container. When you see your seedlings slightly wilted it is time to water again. Also, gently pressing the soil in the top part of the container will tell you if your soil is drying out and if watering is necessary. However, if you are using vermiculite as a growing medium you might be fooled into unnecessary watering because the top part of the medium feels dry while the seedlings' roots are comfortably moist.

If you have sown too many seeds, a common problem, thinning is indispensable. Crowded seedlings will become leggy and won't develop well. Gently pull out the extra seedlings, allowing large-seeded plants about a half inch of space and the small-seeded plants, like celery, about a quarter inch.

Transplanting Indoors

When your seedlings have their first true leaves, they are ready to be transplanted into individual containers. Again, you can use milk cartons, but this time cut them the other way, across the width of the carton about four inches from the bottom. Many other containers will also work well. If you are a recycler at heart, you can collect plastic or styrofoam cups that would otherwise be thrown in the trash. Keep your eyes open at gatherings and parties for wasted cups. Many ready-made containers are on the market. Among them are peat pots (the square ones take less room), compressed peat pellets (Jiffy-7, Jiffy-9), and fiber blocks (Frtl-cubes).

No matter what kind of homemade containers you use, wash them with hot soapy water before using them. Make holes in the bottom for drainage, and add the soil mixture you have selected. Since damping-off does not seriously threaten transplants you can skip the soil pasteurization. And, of course, pure vermiculite as a sterile medium is out of the question.

The size of the containers you select will directly affect the development of the transplants. While yogurt containers suffice for basil or cabbage plants, they are less desirable for peppers and tomatoes. These develop healthier root systems in one-pound cottage cheese containers. By all means, avoid shallow containers. A nine square-inch pot works well for most plants. (If you are using flats be sure the soil is at least three inches deep. And because you transplant more than one seedling into each flat, set the seedlings at least three inches apart.)

Before transplanting, thoroughly water your seedlings. Fill the new containers with the prepared moistened medium. Now, with a fork or spoon, loosen the seedlings, gently lift them out, and separate them. With your index finger punch a hole in the medium to accommodate the roots of one of your seedlings. Pick up the seedling by its new leaves, and place it in the hole, pressing the soil around it. Be careful to not damage the stem while transplanting the plant.

If your seedling has extensive roots, this procedure might crowd the root system. In this case fill your container only half full. Tilt the container, and place the seedling on the slanted surface of the medium. Then cover the roots until the container is filled.

Water your transplanted seedlings, and keep them out of bright light for a couple of days. Exposure to direct light will cause wilting.

Use care when watering; water-logging will harm the seedlings. Feed your plants once a week by adding fish emulsion to the water, three to five tablespoons per gallon. You can also purchase other organic fertilizers to feed your plants.

Hardening-Off

This step prevents plants from being harmed by sudden changes of

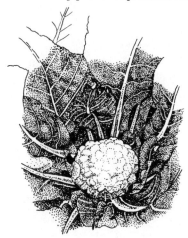

temperature. Ten days before transplanting outdoors to a permanent location, put your plants outside, but not in full sunlight. Begin exposing your plants to full sunlight for an hour per day, and gradually increase the exposure. Finish hardening-off your plants by giving them full exposure to the sun.

Limit watering during the hardening-off period.

If your garden is not in a windy spot, and if your plants are stocky and healthy, you can avoid hardening-off. In any event, do not harden-off plants from the cucurbit family: cucumbers, melons, and squashes.

Transplanting to a Permanent Location

Transplanting brings out a gardener's maternal instincts. This is true when you transplant seedlings, and it is also true when you move plants into their permanent locations. Since the shock of transplanting will slow down your plants' growth, they need delicate handling. Fortunately, normal growth resumes as soon as plants establish their roots in their new environment. Needless to say, a good root system eases the shock of transplanting. You can limit the shock to your plants by following these steps:

- Put seedlings in individual containers instead of flats.
- Transplant in the evening or on a cloudy day; don't transplant in full sun.
- Select plants with stocky stems.
- Choose and prepare a site for your plants in advance.
- Water your plants well after transplanting them.

When transplanting, always dig a hole larger than the root system of the plant. However, some plants need an even more spacious new home, especially tomatoes, peppers, and eggplants. For these plants, dig a hole the depth and width of a shovel, place compost or well-rotted manure on the bottom, set the plant in, fill the hole, and make sure to press the soil snugly around the plant. Since air pockets invite disease, roots must have good contact with the new soil.

If you are using peat pots, remove the bottoms to give the roots more freedom to expand, and be sure to bury the tops of the pots (otherwise, the pots will wick moisture away from your plants' roots). Peat pellets often have a netting around them; make a vertical slit on both sides before you set them in the ground.

At this stage there are two major threats to your transplants: cutworms (which are a particular threat to the cole family) and late frost (which damages tomatoes, peppers, eggplants, and the cucurbits). One way to protect against cutworms is to place a collar around the plants. If you have grown your seedlings in styrofoam cups, cut out the bottom part of the container, leaving the top two inches. Transplant your seedlings with that collar buried one inch in the soil. Cutworms live near the surface of the soil and are not clever enough to reach the plants by crawling under the collar.

You can prevent late frost damage by covering your plants with cardboard boxes, grocery bags (insert two stakes by the plant so the bag will not collapse), a mobile cold frame, or a floating row-cover. (See *Season Extenders*, below.) Be alert to the weather report!

Season Extenders

In cold climates you measure a growing season by the number of frost-free days, a measurement that actually doesn't live up to expectations. An area with many frost-free days but not enough sunshine will make for disappointing gardening, while another area with fewer frost-free days but many sunny days will make for a more successful garden.

Since growing seasons are shorter in the north, gardeners look for ways to prolong them. Fortunately, you can choose from among many season extenders.

Permanent Cold Frames

You can easily make a permanent cold frame with a minimal investment. Cold frames can be used to start seedlings and to grow early crops in the spring or late crops in the fall; especially for greens.

A cold frame is a bottomless wooden box that rests on top of the ground. (See **Appendix II**, page 138, for a source on building and using cold frames.) A frame three by six feet is large enough to grow seedlings for a family of four and can hold ten flats. First find a good south-facing spot in which to locate it, protected from the wind and with no shade trees to interfere with sunlight. If your house has a south-facing wall that you can use, you have the ideal location.

You can build the cold frame with scrap lumber, and the size is up to you. The north-facing side has to be higher than the south by six inches. A standard box is twelve-inches high in front and eighteen-inches in the back. The slope allows for sunshine to reach the plants and for rain to run off.

You can make the lid of the cold frame out of window sashes, storm windows, or a frame you can build yourself and cover with four-mil plastic film. Hinge the lid to the frame, and use weather stripping around it to make the box fairly tight. It is important to keep the warm air in and the cold air out. Mound some dirt around the frame to keep it better insulated. A cold frame's only source of heat is the sun, and thus it is dependent upon weather conditions. To ward off the effects of a cold night, cover the frame with a blanket before the sun goes down. Conversely, if the weather is sunny, the temperature in your cold frame will shoot up. In this case you will need to prop the lid up for ventilation.

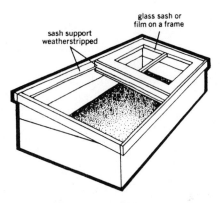

glass sash or film on a frame

sash support weatherstripped

The ideal temperature in a cold frame depends on what you are growing; cool-season seedlings like cabbage and lettuce grow better at temperatures in the 60s, while peppers prefer temperatures in the 70s. You should monitor the temperature inside a cold frame with a thermometer and learn how to control it. A temperature inside a cold frame of 100 degrees F. will be the kiss of death to the plants and your work.

How do you use a cold frame? Gardeners tailor them to fit their particular needs.

Early in the spring, as early as March, you can start greens like lettuce or spinach. You can use cold frames to start seedlings directly, for transplanting of seedlings started indoors, or for hardening-off.

To give warm-weather crops like tomatoes or peppers a head start, put them in your cold frame. Remove or prop open the top of the frame when the plants get too tall and the weather warms up.

For the fall, start a new crop of greens in your cold frame two months before the first frost is expected, and you will have fresh greens until Thanksgiving.

In the winter you can use your cold frame to store root vegetables, properly insulated with leaves or straw. Or you can use the frame to store tools.

Portable Cold Frames

Cold frames do not have to be permanently installed. Portable ones serve different purposes. You can germinate or give a boost to an early planting or protect a late one in any part of your garden. When you want to place the cold frame over another part of your garden, simply pick up the frame, reposition it, and secure it. This type of frame invites ingenuity and is easy to build with scrap material. Make sure to allow for some kind of ventilation for sunny warm days. If you decide on an 'A' frame design, make sure it can be folded for convenient storage.

Hot Beds

A hot bed is a cold frame with a source of heat warming the soil. Two sources of heat you can use are fresh manure and electric cable.

To build a hot bed using manure, first dig a pit two feet deep. Fill the bottom with fresh manure, packing it down as you go along. Fill the last eight inches with soil. The decomposition of the manure will heat the soil.

However, fresh manure is not always available. Electric cable provides an alternative that will bring effective results. (You can buy cable at electrical supply stores, at nurseries, or through a mail-order catalogs.)

Installing cable is easier than digging a manure bed. Simply dig a hole ten to twelves inches deep and spread two inches of sand on the bottom. Place the cable evenly over the surface, then spread another two inches of sand. Cover the sand with a half inch of hardware cloth, then spread the soil. The sand ensures proper drainage to protect the

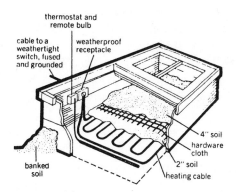

thermostat and remote bulb
cable to a weathertight switch, fused and grounded
weatherproof receptacle
4" soil
hardware cloth
2" soil
banked soil
heating cable

cable, and the hardware cloth protects it from sharp tools when you work in the hot bed.

The cable has a thermostat and will provide a labor-free, warm environment. The ideal temperature for a hot bed is 75 degrees F., but if you want the best of both worlds, you can divide your frame into a hot bed and a cold bed. The hot bed will allow you to grow plants in the fall more dependably. Leafy vegetables will also do well, and you might like to experiment with other crops.

Remember, hot beds do not perform miracles. When severe winter weather sets in, accept your fate. But, thanks to recent technology, gardeners now have ways other than cold and hot frames to extend the spring and fall growing seasons.

Floating Row Covers

Thin, transparent cloth, made out of spun polyester or polyethylene, row covers perform miracles! (Reemay and Agronet are well-known brands.) They are versatile and give spectacular results. Row covers are so light they can be placed directly on freshly seeded or planted areas. As plants grow they push up the material. Since light and rain pass through the covers, they provide labor-free protection. Row covers create a cushion of air between the soil and the ambiant air, providing frost protection down to 27 degrees F. By the same token, this type of insulation speeds the germination of any type of seed; for example, carrots planted under row covers require ten days to germinate instead of the standard twenty days. Finally, when spring brings hungry birds and insects like flea beetles, your crops will grow unblemished.

Row covers can also be used in the summer to protect plants that do not need pollination (cabbage, broccoli, cauliflower, etc.) from cabbage worms. Spinach planted in the fall, or lettuce protected with a row cover over the winter, will surprise you with an extra early yield the following spring.

Wall O'water

This season extender benefits warm season plants like tomatoes, peppers, eggplants, and melons. It is ingenious and made to last for many years. The tepee-shaped device is made out of polyethylene tubes, which you place around your plant and fill with water. When the water warms during the day it creates a microclimate that protects the plants from freezing, even if temperatures drop to 20 degrees F. or below. Seedlings quickly outgrow and are crowded by the Wall o'water, and at that point you should remove it. By then you can expect your crops to be a month ahead.

Tunnels

The easiest season extenders you can build, tunnels are made from four-mil plastic film (lighter film tears too easily).

To make a tunnel, drape clear plastic film over hoops made from either heavy gauge wire or one-inch PVC pipe, depending on how large the tunnel is going to be. Heavy gauge wire from a hardware store is satisfactory for a small tunnel, while one-inch PVC pipe is ideal for a bed. Place a hoop every eighteen to twenty-four inches. Anchor the plastic with anything available—boards or bricks work well. Tunnels offer efficient protection for early spring or fall planting. However, if you expect some sunshine, open both ends of the tunnel, at least partially, before you leave your garden during the day. Without such vigilance you may return to find a crop of cooked lettuce.

You can purchase ready-made tunnels with slit tops that prevent overheating, so you don't have to worry about ventilation.

When To Plant

Vegetables fall into two groups: the cool-season, frost-hardy types and the warm-season types. (See *Varieties for Cold Climates*, page 83 for specifics.) Warm-season vegetables cannot be planted until the soil is thoroughly warm. Usually your soil will be warm enough two weeks after the last spring frost. However, watch the weather. If it has been unusually cool and wet, postpone planting warm-weather vegetables until the soil warms up.

Do not transplant seedlings in direct sunlight; transplant in the evening or on an overcast day. Conversely, sunny days are preferable for planting seeds.

Wait to plant early crops until your soil is neither completely wet nor dry. To check, pick up a handful of soil and squeeze it tightly into a ball. If it holds together and "slicks" when you slide your thumb over it, then it's still too moist. Your soil is ready to plant in when it holds together but crumbles easily when you poke at it.

Don't work the soil in your seed bed until you are ready to plant. Even if you till your entire garden in the spring, you'll need to loosen the soil again just before planting.

If you want straight rows (important only in a small, tight garden) pound a stake at each end of a row, and run a string or rope between the stakes. This way you can make a straight row with no trouble, and the rows will be marked before the seeds sprout.

Check the seed package for the recommended depth to plant the seeds. Generally, seed planting depth is four times the diameter of the seed. If your garden soil tends to cake when it's watered, cover the seeds with finely screened compost instead of dirt. The compost ensures a soft cover for the seeds to push through.

Once you plant the seeds, tamp the soil well. The back of your rake is a good tool for this job. Air between seed and dirt traps bacteria that can rot the seed.

Vegetable	When to Plant Outdoors
Asparagus	2-4 weeks before last spring frost
Beans	1-4 weeks after last spring frost
Beets	2-4 weeks before last spring frost
Broccoli	4-6 weeks before last spring frost
Cabbage	4-6 weeks before last spring frost
Carrots, early	2-6 weeks before last spring frost
Carrots, late	8-10 weeks before first fall frost
Cauliflower	2-4 weeks before last spring frost
Corn	Frost-free date when soil is well warmed
Cucumbers	1 week after last spring frost
Eggplant	1 week after last spring frost
Greens, Chinese	4-6 weeks before last spring frost
Lettuce, early	4-6 weeks before last spring frost
Lettuce, late	6 weeks before first fall frost
Muskmelons	1-2 weeks after last spring frost
Onions	4-6 weeks before last spring frost
Parsnips	2-4 weeks before last spring frost
Parsley	2-4 weeks before last spring frost
Peas	4-6 weeks before last spring frost
Peppers	Frost-free date when soil is well warmed
Potatoes	4-6 weeks before last spring frost
Radishes	2-8 weeks before last spring frost
Rutabaga	4 weeks before last spring frost
Spinach	4-8 weeks before last spring frost
Squash	1-2 weeks after last spring frost
Tomatoes	Frost-free date when soil is well warmed
Turnips	4-6 weeks before last spring frost

Frost-Free Days

Frost-free days for a particular area are the average number of days that temperatures are 32 degrees F. or warmer. (You can find out the number of frost-free days for your area by contacting your county extension agent.) In many cases, freezing or even cooler temperatures will not kill your plants. This means that the growing season can be longer than the number of frost-free days.

Growing seasons differ widely over short distances. When you decide when to plant and when to harvest, take these factors into account: elevation, nearness to rivers or other bodies of water, whether the garden is on the north or south side of a valley, exposure to wind, and your own observations. If a county extension agent is not available to provide you with advice, a library or a National Weather Service office are two good sources of information on your local climate.

Finally, don't forget one of the most reliable sources of information on gardening in your area, especially if you are new gardener—that old timer who is often so willing to tell you what to do and how to do it. Don't overlook such wisdom.

CHAPTER 4

Tending Your Garden

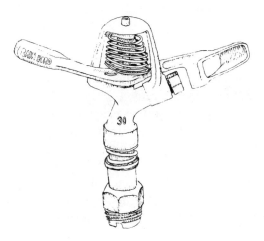

Watering

Your success with any garden depends on how much water is available to your plants. Mother Nature provides or doesn't provide, depending on where you live. In some areas gardeners don't have to worry about watering; in others watering is imperative. Most plants need about an inch of water each week to maintain satisfactory growth. However, take special care with recent transplants; they lose their water-absorbing root hairs and may need up to two inches of water a week. (If you want to know how much water your plants receive, place an empty coffee can in your garden as a gauge.) As a general rule, your garden needs water when the soil is dry three inches below the surface; check with your finger.

How often you need to water depends mostly on the quality of your soil. Sandy soil needs watering more often than heavy loam. The more organic matter your soil contains, the more moisture it will retain.

Gardeners have numerous ways of watering and with time you will develop your own preferred system. The plan of your garden, its size, and what you grow will help you with this decision.

Overhead Watering

Most gardeners prefer this method since the equipment used for the lawn is also used for the garden. Many models of sprinklers are available. The best provide soft watering; heavy overhead watering causes the soil to compact, which is detrimental to good plant growth.

Overhead water in the morning so the plants will dry by nightfall, reducing the possibility of diseases such as mildew. Do not water in the heat of the day; too much water is lost to evaporation and the leaves of certain vegetables can be damaged. Watering in the evening is a water saver but encourages diseases, and pests like slugs can have a heyday.

Soaker Hoses

Made out of rubber, canvas, or plastic, you place soakers between the rows of your garden. Look for a flexible hose since you will have to move it among the plants. Some soakers ooze water, and some squirt water from little holes. Relatively inexpensive, soakers deliver the water directly to the plants. Canvas soakers tend to mold, so use those made from plastic or rubber.

Drip Irrigation

Drip irrigation systems consist of small plastic pipes laid throughout the garden, and, through little holes called "emitters" water is custom-delivered to each plant, drop by drop, over a long period of time. This type of watering ensures the consistent input plants like, prevents caking of the soil, and saves time and water.

The sophistication of your drip system depends on your pocketbook and your determination. But quality is important and determines how well a system works.

While drip systems suit solid-block gardens, they are not so practical for small garden plots placed in different areas of your backyard.

Watering Cans

If your garden is small, you might prefer to water by hand using a watering can fitted with a rose for a rain-like delivery and without a rose for individual plants.

Special Note

Light and frequent watering is acceptable for your plants. Although it encourages plants to develop shallow roots, it also ensures constantly moist soil.

Cultivation

A garden will not grow without help from the gardener. Cultivation is indispensable after your seeds become seedlings. It's time to cultivate when you can see rows of plants.

If you have an older garden and the soil has been worked properly, seedlings will probably emerge first and the weeds later. But weeds grow faster than seedlings regardless of when they appear, and it is imperative to get rid of weeds if you want a productive garden. Cultivation will let your plants get ahead of the weeds.

Cultivation loosens the soil, gives plants some breathing space, and makes it easier for water to penetrate the soil. After a heavy rain or a few overhead waterings, you will notice that the soil begins to cake; a rapid cultivation is now necessary.

The first cultivation should be shallow, so that the small roots of the seedlings will not be disturbed. When the plants are stronger, you can cultivate deeper. Do not cultivate when your plants are wet, especially beans. Thinning your seedlings when you cultivate is also a good idea.

You can cultivate with a hoe or a cultivator. Straddle your row, and cultivate both sides while walking backwards so your steps don't tramp down the area you have just worked. With this system you can cultivate two rows at a time. A cultivator called a potato hook, with four tines, is narrow enough to work between close-together rows. A weeding hoe, with two prongs on one side and a blade on the other, lends itself particularly well to close planting and cultivation.

Thinning

When seeds have performed their miracles by becoming plants, they need room to grow. Each type of plant needs a different amount of elbow room, and it is up to you to make sure it gets the space it needs. Radishes, for instance, will not form a root if left crowded. Again, seed packets give you good general information about thinning. Simply pull your excess plants, trying to pull the ones that look less healthy. (If you want to avoid this chore, you can buy seed tapes where the seeds are pre-spaced for you—convenient for small seeds.)

When you thin, remember that some thinnings make excellent additions to soups, and lettuce thinnings make good early and delicate salads.

Weeding

Chore, battle, war, challenge, relaxation—take your pick. If vegetables had the determination of weeds, our gardening would be too simple. Weeds grow fast and can choke out what you have planted in no time at all. Weed seeds can stay viable for years, just to keep your life busy.

Instead of going at weeding all at once, making it a big job where you can get discouraged, keep it tolerable by doing it as you go along.

Weeds can be kept in check by mulching with grass clippings, straw, hay, or plastic film. (See *Mulching*, page 48.)

Pull your weeds when they are young. Add them to your compost pile, or put them in black plastic bags. Tie them and leave them in a hidden corner of your yard until the following year, when they will have turned into good rich compost.

Eat Your Weeds

Before you pull your weeds you should know that some of them make excellent eating. But before eating any plant, be certain of what you are putting on your dinner table. Several poisonous plants grow in every region.

These three edible weeds commonly grow in gardens.:

Chickweed: A lacy weed with fragile leaves, it has a bland taste and can be used as spinach. Chickweed spreads rapidly if not pulled.

Lamb's Quarter: This vigorous weed is present in almost all gardens. An early-germinating plant, it will give you greens long before anything you plant yourself. Let one plant go to seed in the summer so you can have garden salads first thing the next spring. When picked young, lamb's quarter can be stir-fried, steamed, or tossed in a salad. It tastes similar to spinach and is richer in iron and protein. The plant will grow up to three-feet tall. At that stage only the leaves are edible. You can blanch and freeze them for use in winter soups.

Purslane: This inconspicuous weed crawls between your vegetables and acts as a ground cover. It has oval, slightly succulent leaves. The flowers are yellow and tiny. The leaves and young stems, not the flowers, make an excellent addition to green salads. They have a slightly acidic taste.

Mulching

The pleasure of gardening is often measured by the amount of weeding you don't have to do.

One way to forestall the battle of the weeds is to mulch your garden, creating an organic covering that retains soil moisture, stabilizes soil temperature, improves soil quality, and protects the soil from minor erosion.

As the gardening season passes, you will notice that your mulch disappears. It turns into humus, through natural decomposition or with the help of earthworms. Mulch attracts earthworms, keeping them active through the summer and late fall, after which they usually retreat to deeper soil. Earthworms feed on decomposing organic mulches, eliminating the residue as castings that are rich in nutrients in a form readily available to plants. However, earthworms do not like to feed on two popular mulches: sawdust and pine needles.

Mulching is a personalized gardening technique. Your choice of mulch depends on what material is available to you at an affordable price, plus the type of soil you have and the plants you grow.

Choosing a Mulch

You have two types of mulch to choose from. An insulating mulch reflects heat, keeping the soil cooler during the day and warmer during the night. Insulating mulches include straw, hay, dry leaves, grass clippings, sawdust, and newspaper. A heat conducting mulch warms the soil both day and night by absorbing solar energy. Black plastic film is most commonly used for this purpose.

Plants such as cabbage, potatoes, lettuce, onions, and most root vegetables grow better under insulating mulches. With cabbages, however, wait until the plants are well established before mulching. And keep your mulch from touching the stems of your plants to prevent pest and disease problems.

With potatoes, mulching not only increases the yield, but some evidence suggests that mulched potatoes are less infested by potato bugs, which cannot make their way through the mulch.

When choosing your mulch consider the kind of soil you have. A sandy loam warms up earlier in the spring than a heavy, clayish loam; thus, you don't have to worry about an insulating mulch trapping frost in the ground. If you garden in an area that tends to get water-logged, a mulch cover will be more detrimental then beneficial; it will cut aeration, and plants will rot.

As a rule of thumb, light soils require a thicker layer of mulch than heavy soils to provide the same insulation and water retention. However, heavy soils benefit from the decomposition of thick layers of mulch, since mulches eventually decompose into humus that lightens the soil.

If you practice intensive gardening—in short, spacing your rows much closer together than the seed packets advise—you will find coarse materials like straw difficult to handle; finer materials, like grass clippings or sawdust, are preferable. Coarser materials are better suited to widely spaced rows.

Mulches vary in quality. Remember that any fresh organic mulch will decompose with the help of bacteria. In order to break down the mulch and transform it into humus, bacteria need nitrogen from the soil.

Your soil should have a good supply of nitrogen so that your plants will not suffer as decomposition proceeds. The use of rotted or partially rotted mulches will help prevent nitrogen depletion. Rotted straw, hay, or sawdust, for example, is preferable to fresh. If your mulch is fresh, side dress with manure.

Alfalfa is the king of mulches; it will add nitrogen to your soil. Second to alfalfa are grass clippings, which are also high in nitrogen.

Mulch Materials

Baled hay and straw have an advantage over loose hay or straw because you can peel off easy-to-handle "books" of mulch. Simply place the books between the rows or cover all the soil between the hills. You will find this a convenient way to prevent weeds from coming up in the wide spaces not planted in vegetables. This procedure promptly eliminates most further weeding and cultivation.

Sawdust makes an excellent mulch; it is so fine, one inch should do the job of cutting down the weeds. Sawdust comes in two forms: one is fresh and light in color, the other well rotted and dark. The latter makes a far superior mulch, since it has already begun to decompose.

Dry leaves make good mulch, but use them with caution because they tend to bind together when wet, compressing the soil. After one year, dry leaves become leaf mold, a valuable and rich mulch especially suited to perennials.

Grass clippings are ideal to use after planting, since you can easily get them after spring is under way. An advantage of clippings is that they are easy to handle. You can also add clippings immediately after planting your seeds. Sprinkled sparingly over rows of seeds, they will prevent the soil from forming a crust that is difficult for seeds to push through. Use clippings more generously between rows. As the season progresses, increase the thickness of the mulch; three to four inches of clippings will pack down to about a half inch. Grass clippings tend to be absorbed into the soil shortly after being applied, so you have to replace them frequently. You will also notice that grass clippings quickly dry up under the summer sun.

Be careful with clippings packed in plastic bags. Some will have already begun anaerobic decomposition and will have a moldy appearance. These become quite hot. Decomposing clippings might kill your plants, particularly seedlings, if applied too closely. Be on the safe side and dry these clippings before using them.

Newspapers are an effective and convenient mulch. Apply them about six pages thick between rows. If you think they are unsightly, cover them with a bit of dirt. At the end of the growing season, or the next spring, work the old newspapers into the soil. They will decompose but will not add nitrogen to the soil. Also, use only paper with black ink. Colored print contains toxic chemicals that you do not want to add to your soil.

Black plastic film should be applied with some planning. If you plan to flood irrigate, dig trenches first. If you plan to overhead water, make depressions in the soil where your plants or seeds will go so that both irrigation water and rain water will collect and filter into the soil.

Anchor plastic film by burying the edges in dirt and placing stones at strategic points in the middle.

When planting, cut openings in the plastic by slashing "T"-shaped cross cuts wide enough so the plants will not be rubbed by the edges of the plastic. If you want it to last, use black plastic at least four mil thick. This heavy a plastic will not tear, and you can roll it up at the end of the season to use the following year.

Black plastic warms the soil by absorbing heat. Warm soil benefits vines like cucumbers, cantaloupes, and squash as well as plants like tomatoes, peppers, and eggplants. It also keeps all the weeds out and the moisture in. But, it doesn't decompose and therefore will not add organic material to the soil.

When to Mulch

Your style of gardening dictates when and how to mulch.

You can apply mulch before or after planting. The mulches most commonly applied before planting—but after soil preparation—are hay, straw, or plastic film.

If you apply mulch after planting, wait until the seedlings are well established and you have thoroughly watered and lightly cultivated the soil.

If you want to use an organic insulating mulch on your heat-loving plants like tomatoes, peppers, eggplants, and vines, do so after the blossoms have appeared. An early mulching might delay the setting of fruits by keeping the soil cool. Corn, too, likes heat, and if you decide to mulch it wait until the corn is knee-high. You don't have to wait if you use black plastic; in fact, it will encourage earlier yields by helping warm the soil.

Mulching Your Mulch

As you may expect, mulching requires effort. Mulching breeds mulching. Because of the insulation it provides, mulching encourages plants to develop superficial root systems; these roots do not go deep into the soil to look for moisture. Once you have begun mulching, if you remove the mulch or fail to maintain its thickness, the superficial roots will dry up, checking your plants' growth.

Disease and Pest Control

Although diseases can affect any garden, an organic gardener has less to worry about on this score than a conventional one. A healthy soil, rich in organic matter, provides the best assurance against diseases, and a healthy plant is better equipped to resist them. This is one reason good tilling is an important part of garden management; it provides conditions favorable to vigorous growth.

Climate has a great deal to do with the prevalence of a disease. Hot and dry climates tend to curb diseases, while hot and humid climates tend to provide diseases with more fertile conditions. Finally, severe winters make overwintering of insects and diseases more difficult.

To fight disease, prevention is your most effective tool. Crop rotation is the best control for many common plant diseases. To avoid the cumulative effect of an infection, crops should not be raised in the same location for more than three years. A small garden can be divided into thirds, where you grow vegetables susceptible to diseases on a different plot each year. Follow root crops with leafy vegetable crops, and vice versa. Be careful though; some seemingly different vegetables belong to the same family and should be rotated with vegetables of another family. For instance, tomatoes should not be rotated with eggplants, peppers, or potatoes, since they all belong to the same family.

Talk to your plants! Surely you have heard this saying. It means that a daily stroll in your garden might enable you to detect the beginning of a problem while it is still easy to deal with. This is why having a garden not too far from your house makes it more practical to respond to the needs of your plants.

Blight: Early and late blight have become catch-all terms describing a plant when spots appear on its leaves. For instance, late blight in potatoes will appear shortly after blooming and the plant will then dry up. Different plants have their own blights. Your county extension agent is the best doctor for an accurate diagnosis.

You can prevent or curb blight by using an organic fungicide such as the sulfur-based product Safer offers. Also, destroy seriously diseased plants, do not leave crop residue on your garden after you harvest, practice crop rotation, and select resistant varieties.

Downy mildew: This disease is partial to cucumbers; other vegetables have their own forms of mildew. Unlike powdery mildew, downy mildew causes the older underleaves to become brown and die. This disease is caused by a fungus that does not overwinter in cold climates. However, wind will bring it back the next growing season.

Fusarium wilt: This soil-borne fungus attacks the roots, preventing them from absorbing water and thereby causing the plant to wilt. Yellowing of the lower leaves is the first symptom, and death follows. The only effective prevention this disease—which is partial to peas, tomatoes, potatoes, and cucumbers—is to select resistant varieties, and practice crop rotation. Fusarium wilt is persistent and overwinters in the debris of your garden.

Mosaic: This virus causes mottling of cucumber and squash leaves. Plants become stunted and the fruits will become oddly shaped. Using mosaic resistant varieties is the best way to avoid this disease.

Nematodes: Nematodes live in all soils, but these extremely small parasites wreak havoc only when weather conditions are just right. The nematodes will then pierce the roots, form knots, and diminish a plant's ability to get nutrients from the soil. The plant will become stunted and in some instances die. A soil rich in nutrients is the best deterrent to nematodes. Organic matter is rich in fungi that, in turn, parasitize nematodes.

Powdery mildew: This white powder forms on pea plants and pods, cucumbers, beans, and squash and is invasive. Overhead watering worsens an infestation. If you choose to overhead water, be sure to water during the day and not in the evening. Powdery mildew usually appears toward the end of a crop and is not a major menace. As soon as harvesting is finished, dig up the plants to prevent spreading the disease.

Root rot: This disease is also partial to peas and is confused with Fusarium wilt. However, root rot appears at flowering time, when the plant becomes yellow and dies. Too much moisture causes the disease to spread; with good drainage it should not occur.

Scab: This common potato disease is cosmetic and does not affect the taste. Scabs that form on the tubers can be isolated or cover the whole potato, according to the degree of the infection. Since the fungi is soil-borne, rotate potato planting sites, use certified seed potatoes, and plant resistant varieties.

Verticulium wilt: The disease shows the same symptoms as fusarium wilt, but the plant does not die; the plant's growth slows. This fungus is more prevalent where the climate is cool and rainy.

Resistant varieties

A gardener can prevent disease problems by selecting resistant varieties. Letters following the name of a variety on seed packets and in catalogs indicate the kind of resistance. For example:

V = resistance to verticulium wilt
F = resistance to fusarium wilt
N = resistance to nematodes

Non-diseases

Blossom-end Rot: Not actually a disease, blossom-end rot is a response to a stressful condition. A dark-brown sunken spot at the end of a tomato indicates that the plant has been subjected to prolonged water starvation. Even and regular watering is the best preventative.

Cracking: Too much moisture causes tomatoes to grow too fast. If too much water is followed by a dry spell, cracking of the fruit often results. Varieties with smaller fruits are less susceptible; for varieties with large fruits look for those described as resistant to cracking. Even watering also helps prevent cracking.

Sunscald: This condition affects tomatoes and peppers. A whitish area appears, becomes leathery, and rot eventually follows. Again, this is not a disease but simply the result of fruits not having adequate protection from the sun. Heavy pruning of a tomato plant invites this condition. Where the sun is fierce, select varieties with good foliage protection.

Additional advice

- Don't be discouraged by this list of diseases and stress-caused problems. Often what looks like disease might simply be leaves damaged by rain, wind, or too much sunshine.

- If your compost pile doesn't heat up to 160 degrees F., do not compost diseased plants or keep them around your garden.

- Do not walk in your garden when the plants are wet: if a disease is present, you could be helping spread it around.

- Remember, your best measure against disease is prevention through sanitation and crop rotation.

Insect pests and their control

Don't panic at the sight of a few bugs. Before you invest in insect controls, wait and see which problems are solved by natural predators and hand picking. It is foolish to expect a pest-free garden; that would deprive your predators of food, and some predators are fun to watch in action. Certainly you enjoy the swooping flight of a swallow! Do not forget to trim your vegetable garden with flowers. Flowers are more than pretty; they provide an attractive environment for some helpful predators.

Aphids

Common and stubborn, aphids are a sucking-type pest—the lice of the plant kingdom. They are small, and their color varies from green to gray to red. They go through a cycle from wingless to winged insect and back again, spawning many generations, each with different eating habits. Different generations of aphids feed on different plants. This highly adaptable pest clusters under the leaves and on the stems, weakening the plant.

If you notice curled leaves on your plants, look for aphids. If you see ants busily moving up and down a tree or plant, you know colonies of aphids are to be found. Aphids excrete honeydew, which is nectar to ants. Ants farm aphids to support their vice.

Aphids shy away from strong and healthy plants. Soil rich in organic matter also works as a deterrent. Aphids prefer to feed on weak plants or plants that do not get enough water. Ideally, you won't have an aphid problem if your garden is well tended. But an onslaught of aphids must be dealt with.

Fortunately, you can effectively combat aphids. Spray your plants with a strong stream of water. This will knock the aphids to the ground, where they will get stuck in the mud.

Ladybugs prey upon aphids; they eat many times their weight in the pests. (You can buy ladybugs from your local nursery or through seed catalogs.) In the evening release a few ladybugs at a time at the bottom of your plants. With their voracious appetites they will eat their way up the plant.

Insecticidal soaps also effectively control aphids.

As a last resort, rotenone powder or spray effectively controls aphids. (See **Bug Eat Bug**, page 61, and **Organic Insecticides**, page 62.)

Cabbage Butterfly, Cabbage Worms

If your cabbage survives the diseases and pests that attack it when it is young, a new menace waits for it when it comes of age: pretty white butterflies. These butterflies like to hover over the cabbage patch and lay their eggs on the underside of the cabbage leaves. These eggs are difficult to locate, but if you do, squash them without shame. If they hatch into green worms, you'll notice their handiwork; they will eat the leaves and even gnaw into the cabbage itself.

Cabbage worms match the green color of cabbage leaves, making them difficult to see. The cabbage looper, also a green worm, has a brown moth for parents. Infestations of either pest never become serious if you control them early. You can easily pick off the worms by hand, especially if you do not have many plants. However, if this repulses you, treating the plants with rotenone or

Thuricide eliminates the problem. A physical barrier, for example spreading a light row cover over your cabbage patch, prevents infestations. Finally, kale, with its crinkly leaves, does not attract the butterflies and can substitute for cabbage.

Cutworms

If you see a cabbage, or any other plant, laying on the ground with its stem chewed through, you can immediately suspect cutworms. Dig gently at the base of the plant, and if you find a grayish, plump worm about one inch long that coils when touched, you know you've got cutworms. They should be killed on sight. And, if you find one, you can assume that you have more of them hiding in your soil.

A garden recently worked from sod has a better chance of cutworm infestation. Since the cutworm moth lays its eggs on grass, keep your garden free of grassy weeds. Cutworms prefer to attack seedlings, especially cabbages, and tomatoes.

Protect your young plants with small cans with the tops and bottoms cut out; set them over the plants, buried an inch in the ground. Similar collars can be made out of cardboard; they should be buried one inch deep also.

Here is another simple trick: plant a toothpick next to your seedling. When the cutworm curls around the stem to feast, the feel of the toothpick will be unpleasant enough to chase it away.

Sweet-Corn Earworm

Rarely does a corn patch make it through the season untouched by earworms. The moth lays eggs on the silk, the whitish or greenish worms feed on the silk and work their way through the husks to the top of the corn cob. One good way to stop them is to drown them in mineral oil. About one week after the silk appears, squirt some oil inside it with a medicine dropper, or any other squeeze-type container. After the silk has wilted apply a few more drops on top of each cob. Spraying with *Bacillus thuringiensis* also effectively rids corn of earworms.

Flea Beetles

These tiny brown or black insects jump away when you touch an infested plant. You can easily identify them by their eating habits; they leave behind a shotgun pattern of little holes in the leaves. The holes weaken the plant but rarely kill it.

Flea beetles prefer radish and turnip greens, as well as tomato, eggplant, and potato plants. Repeated cultivation helps curb the population. You can also use rotenone or pyrethrum for effective control. When pollination of your plants is not necessary, you can prevent infestations by covering your crop with a light row cover.

Good sanitation at the end of the growing season is important; do not leave debris around since the flea beetles will use this as a breeding ground.

Grasshoppers

Most grasshoppers feed on any available vegetation. A good crop of grasshoppers can ruin an entire garden. High weeds near your garden give grasshoppers a good reason to hang around.

Grasshoppers lay their eggs during the fall, in soil not covered by vegetation. If your soil is mulched they prefer going elsewhere. You can limit next year's grasshopper infestation by curbing the hatching of their eggs with a fall tillage; this exposes the eggs to the drying action of sun, wind, and cold. Spring tillage is also effective.

If you have chickens, let them run loose to feed on grasshoppers. Birds also think grasshoppers are a real treat and do an excellent job of controlling them. Why not build the birds some houses and invite them to stay!

A serious infestation of grasshoppers can be treated with grasshopper spores (available in most nurseries). Mechanical controls such as a solution of molasses and water (ten parts of water to one part of molasses) placed in a large container, half-filled, also work to rid your garden of these pests.

Finally, if you do not want grasshoppers to eat your fall crop, you can cover the crop with a floating row cover such as Reemay.

Leafhoppers

These wedge-shaped green insects have a taste for many plants. They suck the underleaves and weaken the plant. When disturbed they hop away. They also transmit diseases to plants; they are not welcome guests!

Rotenone and Pyrethrum provide good control of leafhoppers.

Gophers

If you spot tell-tale mounds and your roots crops start disappearing, you'll have to drive these little guys away. If you don't want to use traps, some seed catalogs offer a deterrent; a device that sends vibrations into the soil and encourages Mister Gopher to go elsewhere. But be forewarned: these devices are expensive!

Onion Maggots

First, a fly that looks like a house fly lays its eggs on your onions. Then the onion tops begin to dry, and the bulb rots. Don't hesitate! Pull out the drying onion immediately. You need to eliminate the eggs.

Try to plant your onions in more than one spot to create diversions for this fly. Add sand or wood ash to the surface of your soil around the onions as a repellent.

Potato Bugs or Colorado Potato Beetles

A large potato patch infested with potato bugs spells a continuous battle for the organic gardener. The first sign of trouble is usually a brown and white striped beetle. Hand pick and destroy that beetle to prevent it from laying eggs. But you may be too late. Check the underside of your potato leaves for clusters of yellow eggs that look like patches of confetti. These clusters of eggs should be crushed. If the eggs have hatched, the bugs have entered the larva state. The larvae have orange, soft bodies with black stripes and should be handpicked and dropped into a can containing some kerosene. The larvae you miss will feed on potato leaves for about three weeks. Then they will bury themselves into the ground, emerging as beetles about ten days later to start another cycle.

According to some people, mulching potatoes with straw after planting efficiently controls the beetles, because the plant can cut through the mulch but the beetle larvae can't.

Dusting with rotenone or *Bacillus thuringiensis* (variety, san diego) also effectively controls the beetle.

Slugs

Slugs are not insects but recalcitrant, tenacious, voracious pests, a force to reckon with, and one that loves lettuce.

Since gardens are moist, they provide a perfect habitat for slugs. They provide an even better haven when mulched with organic matter.

You can trap slugs by placing a shingle or a board set over their paths. After their nocturnal rounds, the slugs will hide in the cool spot under the shingle or board, where you can find them. This method works better in an unmulched garden.

For the mulched garden you can use a different kind of trap. It seems slugs have a vice—they like beer! Place a shallow container of beer on the ground. Level the edges with the ground so the slugs have easy access. They will drown in their vice. However, if you notice that you have a fair number of ground beetles as victims, you face a dilemma. Then, slug saloons, available in nurseries and designed to trap only slugs, are advisable as containers for the beer or other bait you choose.

You can also create your own slug bait out of weeds. You will soon discover slug favorites. Strew a few weeds in your paths. You will notice that the slugs go after the wilted plants before they go after your lettuce. Collect the weeds and slugs early in the morning and discard them in a place where the slugs have no hope of return.

Diatomaceous earth, frequently applied, curbs slug populations. It can be applied around plants or dusted on them. Slugs are soft-bodied and do not like to crawl over anything abrasive. Therefore diatomaceous earth or even a ring of sand around your plants creates an uncomfortable situation for the slugs. Using wood ashes around your plants brings similar results with an additional benefit. Wood ashes will make your soil more alkaline, which is exactly what slugs dislike; they proliferate in acid soil.

If slugs become too great a problem, you can discourage them by modifying your planting methods. You can use elevated rows or narrow beds and water by irrigating, rather than overhead sprinkling. The soil surface around the plants will be dry while the roots will be watered. Needless to say, any other type of watering should be done during the day, not in the evening; offering moisture at night is like creating a heaven for slugs.

Hand-picking slugs might sound repulsive, but it is an effective tactic. The best time to pick slugs is at dusk or early in the morning. Drop the slugs in salted water. If you don't want to deal with slimy creatures, arm yourself with a pair of scissors, and cut the slugs in half. Sweet revenge!

Wireworms
These like to feast on potatoes. To be free of them, place pieces of old potatoes next to the potato patch where the wireworms will find them. Then,

simply dispose of the infested pieces and replace them with more pieces of old potatoes.

Besides potatoes, wireworms attack other vegetables such as onions, beets, carrots, and beans. Practice crop rotation to reduce the threat of these pests. A new garden (replacing sod) or one with poorly drained soil is more susceptible to wireworms.

Bug Eat Bug

You can take several more preventive measures to avoid bug infestations in your garden. Bringing in more bugs and protecting the beneficial bugs you already have are two such measures.

Aphid Lion or Lacewing Fly

Lacewings work as all-purpose predators. Lacewing larvae eat insects voraciously. They destroy aphids, whiteflies, thrips, and spider mites. In its adult stage the lacewing is a light green insect with pale green transparent wings. It feeds on nectar and honeydew. After three weeks a larva becomes an adult, so more than one release of lacewing eggs is necessary for satisfactory control. Lacewings are available through gardening catalogs.

Ladybugs

Adult and larval ladybugs are equally good predators for aphids, scale insects, leafhoppers, mites, corn earworms, red spiders, the eggs of Colorado beetles, and many other bugs.

Ladybugs can be purchased in half-pint or pint containers. The average garden (up to 2,500 square feet) needs no more than a half pint, which contains about 3,000 ladybugs. They can be purchased by mail or from a local nursery, where they are kept in a dormant state. Keep them in a refrigerator until it is time to release them. Set them free in the evening, when the temperature is cool, near the area where the pests are causing problems.

You don't need to release all the ladybugs at one time. Some gardeners find them fickle because they fly away; indeed, if you do not have enough pests to feed their voracious appetites they will move on to greener pastures. But, the larva of the ladybug is even more hungry for aphids than the adult. If the ladybugs have enough food, they will provide your garden with one or more generations of larvae, continually eating your pest problems.

Ground Beetles

A nocturnal insect predator, the ground beetle (also called the calosoma beetle) is easy for you to recognize as it works in your garden. When you see a long, oval-shaped beetle, dull black, brown or metallic green, scurrying by and looking busy, you know it is a ground beetle. Beetles and their larvae feed on cutworms, caterpillars, grasshopper eggs, and many other insects—true friends.

Syrphid Flies

These are commonly called "hover flies," because of their peculiar way of flying over flowers, hovering. They have a wasp-like appearance, with bright yellow and black colors, but they do not sting. Their larvae feed on aphids. Plant flowers to encourage the flies to stay around.

Trichogramma Wasps

These tiny, parasitic insects can barely be seen but are efficient predators in spite of their size. They do not kill their prey immediately, but, instead, lay their eggs in the bodies of insect pests. The Trichogramma wasps effectively control many pests, among them the cabbageworm, cankerworm, corn earworm, tent caterpillar, codling moth, and cutworm. These wasps are sold in vials through mail order catalogs and should be released two or three times, at regular intervals, during the growing season. You have to reintroduce them each year.

Organic Insecticides

If you must use an insecticide, you should be aware of the consequences. Thuricide will kill your cabbage worms without poisoning all your insects or birds. But rotenone will destroy insects indiscriminately, will kill fish, and should be used only as a last resort.

Diatomaceous Earth

Fossilized diatom shells are finely milled to produce diatomaceous earth. When soft-bodied insects come in contact with the microscopic needles of the silica their bodies are punctured, causing dehydration and death. This product effectively kills slugs, cutworms, and root maggots. Beneficial earthworms are not affected.

Grasshopper Spore

Sold as Grasshopper Attack, the spores (*Nosema locustae*) effect grasshoppers but do not harm other insects, birds, animals, plants, or humans. Grasshoppers ingest the spores, become sick, eat less, and then die. Those that do not die carry the infection to other grasshoppers. The full effect of this biological control is better noticed the following season.

Insecticidal Soaps

Safer's soap is readily available at nurseries and gardening supply stores. It is safe, mild, and leaves no residue. It can be applied up to harvest time to control aphids, whiteflies, leafhoppers, and spider mites. To protect bees it is better to spray in the evening.

Reuters makes an insecticidal soap effective for aphids, mites, and other sucking insects.

Organic Fungicide

Safer's fungicide controls fungus diseases, like powdery mildew, black spot and rust, quite well. The active ingredient is sulfur. When the fungicide is applied, the leaves are covered with a film that prevents the disease from taking hold.

Pyrethrum

This insecticide, made from the ground dried flowers of the Dalmatian daisy (*Chrysanthemum cinearaefolium*), is sold alone or added to other products.

Like rotenone, it effectively kills a wide range of sucking and chewing insects and is non-toxic for humans and animals. Rotenone and pyrethrum should be applied late in the evening when bees are inactive. Be aware that pyrethrum, like rotenone, is harmful to fish.

You can prepare your own pyrethrum spray by growing the daisies in your garden. Mix one tablespoon of freshly ground dried flowers with two quarts of hot water. Let the mixture seep for a couple of hours, strain, and add one tablespoon of dish soap. Use immediately.

Be aware that the painted daisy, although called a pyrethrum, belongs to a different species. You can use the flowers to make an insecticidal spray, but it will be much weaker. Painted daisies come in beautiful pink, red, and white blossoms, while the Dalmatian daisy is white.

Rotenone

This insecticide, made from the roots of two tropical plants that contain the active agent, can be used as a dust or a spray. It comes in one- and five-percent concentrations. It effectively kills various insects: aphids, cabbage worms, other kinds of caterpillars, squash bugs, flea beetles, thrips, potato bugs, asparagus beetles, and leafhoppers. In fact, rotenone does not distinguish between good and bad bugs—they are all destroyed on contact.

Rotenone does not harm humans or animals. Vegetables can be eaten one day after being sprayed with it. But be careful with rotenone near water; it is death to fish. Remember, it indiscriminately kills bugs and should be used only if absolutely necessary.

Thuricide or Dipel

This biological insecticide uses *Bacillus thuringiensis* as its active agent. The *Bacillus*, sprayed on plant leaves, paralyzes the intestinal tract of certain insects that consume it, causing the pests to starve to death. *Bacillus thuringiensis* is effective only on caterpillars like cabbage worms and loopers, corn earworms, fruit tree leaf rollers. Since it does not harm animals, humans, birds, bees, or fish, it is a safe insecticide. You can use it up to harvest time.

On the market, Thuricide is a liquid concentrate and Dipel a powder; the latter has a more dependable shelf life.

A new variety of *Bacillus thuringiensis* is now available to combat the Colorado potato beetle. It has to be applied at hatching stage when the larvae are small.

* * *

All the organic insecticides listed are available from nurseries, seed catalogs, and some hardware stores.

Companion Planting

We have no widely accepted scientific explanation for why companion planting works. "Carrots and dill dislike each other," is typical of companion planting advice.

Despite the lack of scientific explanation, many gardeners swear by companion planting. Experience shows that certain plants grow best when planted with certain others. And insects cause less trouble when certain plants grow together in the garden.

Design your own companion garden by using the following charts. The first chart lists crops that get along and don't get along. The second chart lists herbs and describes their beneficial effects on your garden.

To get you started, just remember that cucumbers like peas, peas like beans, and beans like potatoes. But potatoes don't like cucumbers. Make sense?

Vegetable Companion

CROP	LIKES AND DISLIKES
Asparagus	*likes:* Tomatoes, parsley, basil
Beans	*like:* Potatoes, carrots, cucumbers, cauliflower, cabbage, summer savory *dislike:* Onions, garlic, gladiolus
Pole beans	*like:* Corn, summer savory *dislike:* Onions, beets, sunflower
Bush beans	*like:* Potatoes, cucumbers, corn, strawberries, celery, summer savory *dislike:* Onions
Beets	*like:* Onions, kohlrabi *dislike:* Pole beans
Cabbage family	*likes:* Aromatic herbs, potatoes, camomile, peppermint, sage, celery, rosemary, beets, onions *dislikes:* Strawberries, tomatoes, pole beans
Carrots	*like:* Peas, leaf lettuce, chives, leeks, onions, rosemary, sage, tomatoes *dislike:* Dill
Celery	*likes:* Leek, tomatoes, bush beans, cauliflower, cabbage
Chives	*like:* Carrots *dislike:* Peas, beans
Corn	*likes:* Potatoes, cucumbers, peas, beans, pumpkin, squash
Cucumber	*likes:* Beans, corn, peas, radishes, sunflowers *dislikes:* Aromatic herbs, potatoes
Eggplant	*likes:* Beans
Leek	*likes:* Onions, celery, carrots

Planting Chart

CROP	LIKES AND DISLIKES
Lettuce	*likes:* Carrots, radishes, (lettuce, carrots, and radishes make a strong team together), strawberries, cucumbers
Onion & garlic	*like:* Beets, strawberries, tomatoes, lettuce, camomile, summer savory *dislike:* Peas, beans
Parsley	*likes:* Tomatoes, asparagus
Peas	*likes:* Carrots, turnips, radishes, cucumbers, beans, most vegetables and herbs *dislikes:* Onions, garlic, gladiolus, potatoes
Potato	*likes:* Beans, corn, cabbage, horseradish (should be planted at corner of patch), marigold, egg plant *dislikes:* Pumpkin, squash, cucumber, sunflower, tomatoes, raspberry
Pumpkin	*likes:* Corn *dislikes:* Potatoes
Radish	*likes:* Peas, nasturtium, lettuce, cucumbers
Spinach	*likes:* Strawberries
Squash	*likes:* Nasturtium, corn
Strawberries	*like:* Bush beans, spinach, borage, lettuce (as a border) *dislike:* Cabbage
Sunflower	*likes:* Cucumbers *dislikes:* Potatoes
Tomato	*likes:* Chives, onion, parsley, asparagus, marigold, carrots, nasturtium *dislikes:* Kohlrabi, potatoes, fennel, cabbage
Turnip	*likes:* Peas

Herb Companion

HERB	COMPANION AND EFFECTS
Basil	Companion to tomatoes; improves growth and flavor. Repels flies and mosquitoes. Dislikes rue intensely.
Beebalm	Companion to tomatoes; improves growth and flavor.
Borage	Companion to tomatoes, squash, and strawberries; improves growth and flavor. Deters tomato worms.
Caraway	Plant here and there; loosens soil.
Catnip	Plant in borders; deters flea beetle.
Camomile	Companion to cabbages and onions; improves growth and flavor.
Chervil	Companion to radishes; improves growth and flavor.
Chives	Companion to carrots; improves growth and flavor. Repels aphids.
Dead nettle	Companion to potatoes; improves growth and flavor. Deters potato bug.
Dill	Companion to cabbage; improves growth and flavor. Dislikes carrots.
Fennel	Plant away from gardens; most plants dislike it.
Flax	Companion to carrots, potatoes; improves growth and flavor. Deters potato bug.
Garlic	Plant near roses, raspberries, and throughout the garden; improves growth and health. Deters Japanese beetle and flea beetles from potatoes.
Horseradish	Plant at corners of potato patch to deter potato bug.
Henbit	General insect repellent.
Hyssop	Deters cabbage moth; companion to cabbage and grapes. Keep away from radishes.
Lamb's quarter	Allow this edible weed to grow in moderate amounts in the garden, especially in corn.
Lemon balm	Sprinkle throughout garden.
Lovage	Plant here and there; improves flavor and health of plants.
Marigolds	Plant throughout the garden; discourages Mexican bean beetles, nematodes and other insects. The workhorse of pest deterrents.
Mint	Companion to cabbage and tomatoes; improves health and flavor. Deters white cabbage moth.

Planting Chart

HERB	COMPANION AND EFFECTS
Marjoram	Plant here and there in garden; improves flavors.
Mole plant	Plant here and there; deters moles and mice.
Nasturtium	Companion to radishes, cabbage. Plant under fruit trees. Deters aphids, squash bugs, striped pumpkin beetles. Also attracts aphids, luring them away from other crops. Improves growth and flavor.
Petunia	Protects beans. Good for all the garden.
Pot marigold	(Calendula) Companion to tomatoes. Plant here and there in the garden. Deters asparagus beetle, tomato worm, and general garden pests.
Purslane	This edible weed makes a good ground cover for corn.
Pigweed	One of the best weeds for drawing in nutrients. Especially beneficial to potatoes, onions, and corn. Keep thinned.
Peppermint	Companion to cabbage. Repels white cabbage butterfly.
Rosemary	Companion to cabbage, beans, carrots, and sage. Deters cabbage moth, bean beetles, and carrot fly.
Rue	Companion to roses and raspberries. Deters Japanese beetle. Keep away from sweet basil.
Sage	Companion to cabbage and carrots. Deters cabbage moth and carrot fly.
Southernwood	Companion to cabbage; improves growth and flavor. Plant here and there in garden. Deters beetles.
Sowthistle	This weed, in moderate amounts, helps tomatoes, onions, and corn.
Summer savory	Companion to beans and onions; improves growth and flavor. Deters bean beetles and flea beetles.
Tansy	Companion to roses and raspberries. Plant under fruit trees. Deters flying insects, Japanese beetles, striped cucumber beetles, squash bugs, and ants.
Tarragon	Plant throughout garden.
Thyme	Plant here and there in garden; deters cabbage worm.
Valerian	Good anywhere in garden.
Winter savory	General insect repellent.
Wormwood	Plant as a border. Keeps animals from garden.
Yarrow	Companion to aromatic herbs; enhances essential oil production. Plant along borders and paths.

Fall Garden Care

Fall is the time to prepare your perennials—chives, asparagus, mint, etc.—for the winter. After frost has penetrated about an inch below the soil surface, mulch around your plants four to six inches deep. Use light materials such as straw, manure, leaves, or peat moss.

As soon as your corn, squash, beans, and cucumbers finish bearing, pull up the stalks and vines and put them in the compost pile. Composting should kill the eggs of many pests and make controlling them easier next year.

Be sure to cut all weeds before they go to seed. Remember, "One year's seeding makes seven years' weeding." Weeds, leaves, everything you've cleaned out of your flower beds and garden, should go into the compost heap.

Planning Next Year's Garden

Keeping records, noting what varieties did well for you—becoming your own experimental station—is part of gardening. You don't have to be highly scientific; what works best for you is what counts.

When, after a long summer, you put your garden to bed, take the time to plan next year's garden based on your newly acquired experience.

CHAPTER 5

Harvesting

For the home gardener, harvesting suggests fresh vegetables that can be eaten immediately, or processed and stored. Vegetables should be picked at their prime, not too young when the taste is not fully developed nor too old when the taste is poor. Fortunately, the proper time to harvest is easy to learn. You will come to pick vegetables to fit your needs by watching, tasting, and smelling them.

To preserve the vitamin C content of your vegetables, don't harvest before about 10 a.m. Sunshine is essential for plants to produce vitamin C, so it is preferable to harvest after a spell of clear weather. Vegetables, especially leafy kinds, have a tendency to lose vitamin C in storage; when weather conditions permit, they should be freshly picked for the table.

Sweet-tasting vegetables, like peas and corn, should be harvested before their sugar converts to starch. Don't leave them at room temperature, even for a short time, before eating them.

Preparing Storage Space

You can store vegetables indoors or outdoors. If you choose to leave them outdoors in the garden, see *The All-Year Garden*, page 75.

Although most basements are too dry and warm to store most vegetables, they are suitable for onions, garlic, shallots, and tomatoes. But you can modify a heated basement for storage of other vegetables and fruits. Build a partition in your basement, insulating the walls and ceiling of the storage room. The room should also have a window on the outside wall for proper ventilation, maintaining a temperature between 32 and 40 degrees F. The room should be equipped with slatted shelves and flooring to ensure air circulation through the stored items. Since most fruits and vegetables dry out without some moisture in the air, spread an absorbent material, such as dampened sawdust, on the floor.

Cellars under houses without central heat have long been used for winter storage of fruits and vegetables in colder climates. These cellars usually have an outside entrance. The door is a means of ventilating the cellar and regulating the temperature.

Inspect your house. You might find a spot where the temperature is adequate for fruit and vegetable storage during the winter. But, if storage facilities are not practical in the house, you can still store your produce outside, using insulated barrels buried partially in the ground. For more information, and other ideas, consult your county extension service where you can find information and bulletins on how to build good, simple storage space.

Picking and Storing

Beans and Peas

You can store all kinds of dry beans and peas, including lima beans and soybeans, for home use. You can dry beans and peas in two ways. Either pick the pods as soon as they are mature and spread them in a warm, dry place until they are thoroughly dry, or pull and dry the whole bean plant after most of the pods are ripe.

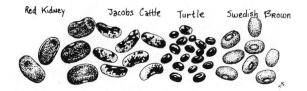

Red Kidney   Jacobs Cattle   Turtle   Swedish Brown

After drying the beans, shell them. One simple method is to put them in a gunny sack or any heavy plastic bag, and then trample them. To separate the chaff from the beans wait for a windy day. Then, take a handful of beans and let them drop slowly onto a blanket. The wind will blow the chaff away.

Onions

Onions must be mature and thoroughly dry to store well. Damaged onions and onions with thick necks will not keep well.

Store onions in a well-ventilated place. Keep them in open containers, such as slatted crates or open mesh bags. Fill the bags half full and hang them on overhead hooks. Or, gather a dozen onions by their necks, tie the necks together and hang. Then just pull your onions from their bundle when you need them.

Peppers

Mature green bell peppers can be kept in home storage for two or three weeks if you handle them properly. Firm, dark-green peppers store best.

Pick all your peppers just before you expect a frost. Wash and sort them according to maturity and firmness. They should be stored in a cool, moist place. To maintain high humidity, put the peppers in a dark plastic bag (such as a trash can liner) with twelve to fifteen holes in it. Then place the bag in a box.

Remember that green peppers are one of the few vegetables that do not need to be blanched before freezing. However, frozen peppers tend to become soft when thawed and are better used for cooking.

Hot peppers are easiest to store after they are dry. You can either pull the whole plant and hang it, or you can pick the peppers off the plant and string them on a line.

Store dry peppers in a cool, dry place, such as an attic or unheated room. They also keep well in brown paper sacks, which are porous enough to allow adequate ventilation.

Potatoes
Potatoes you want to store require special handling at harvest time. Potato vines should be dead at least two weeks before you dig the tubers. Dig the potatoes carefully, and remove them as quickly as possible to prevent sun and wind damage. Do not wash the potatoes, just rub off the dirt and let them cure for two weeks in a dry place away from the sun. Do not store bruised potatoes.

Potatoes will remain firm in storage at temperatures between 35 and 45 degrees F. Higher temperatures will induce sprouting. Potatoes should also be stored in the dark, since light will cause their flesh to turn green and a bitter taste to develop.

If you don't have cool storage in your basement, you can use window wells about two feet below ground level. Place the potatoes in the well, and insulate them. Newspapers or a plastic bag filled with well-packed dry leaves work well. This type of protection relies on your ingenuity and what you have available in your house.

Pumpkins and Squashes
With proper care, hard-rind varieties of pumpkins and winter squash keep for several months. Harvest before frost and leave a piece of stem on them. Only mature fruit free of insect and physical damage should be kept for storage.

Pumpkins and squash keep better if you cure them for ten days at about 80 degrees F.; this hardens their rinds. You can put them near a furnace or heater to cure them. However, don't cure acorn squash before storage. Its flesh turns orange, loses moisture, and becomes stringy.

Store pumpkins and squash at slightly below room temperature, 50 to 60 degrees F. Basements are usually ideal. Do not store them in outdoor cellars.

Tomatoes

With special care, tomatoes can be stored for at least four to six weeks.

Harvest your tomatoes just before the first killing frost. If an unexpected frost occurs, undamaged tomatoes can be salvaged and ripened indoors. Mature green tomatoes will ripen well but immature ones will shrivel. Before storing, wash the fruits in a weak bleach solution (one tablespoon per gallon of water), and dry the tomatoes.

To store green tomatoes, wrap them individually in newspaper and pack them, one or two layers deep, in shallow boxes. This helps prevent any rot from spreading. However, since the tomatoes are wrapped it is difficult to see which ones are rotting. Placing tomatoes on newspaper, close together but not touching, and covering them with several more layers of newspaper, makes checking simple. Lift the top layer and discard decaying fruits.

The easiest way to mature green tomatoes is to pull the entire plant and hang the vines upside down in the basement, where the fruits will ripen without fuss.

Green tomatoes ripen well at room temperature and in the dark. Sunlight is not necessary, which means that you don't need to line up your tomatoes on window sills. Once your tomatoes are ripe, you can hold them in storage at 55 degrees F. By and large, how well ripened tomatoes hold depends on the variety. Meaty fruit have an advantage over juicy ones, and varieties like Long Keeper keep well until March with minimal decay.

The All-Year Garden

Many of us picture a garden as little more in the winter than frost-whitened vines and the skeletal remains of last summer's salads. But for those who don't own a freezer, or don't want to invest money and time in canning, that same frozen plot can provide many fresh vegetables in the dead of winter.

Most root vegetables, such as carrots, beets, rutabagas , turnips, and parsnips, can be left in the ground in the fall, covered with leaves or bales of old straw. Whatever you use, make sure that your vegetable rows are well covered. Bags of leaves or straw can be

placed lengthwise or crosswise with the row, depending on how you have planted your vegetables. Cover all vegetables well and not until after a good frost—otherwise they will rot under the cover.

Where wind-chill factor is a problem, bags alone are not enough. Scatter a good layer of loose leaves over the bags for additional insulation and secure them with a cover (you don't want the neighbors to receive a shower of leaves with the first wind).

With similar protection, you can leave some leafy vegetables—Brussels sprouts, kale, collards, and leeks—in the garden for winter eating. For protection, sandwich the rows between bales of straw or plastic bags filled with leaves. Then when you're ready, just brush snow off the vegetables and pick away.

If you can preserve a delicate vegetable like Brussels sprouts this way, you have truly outsmarted winter. Pick the loose sprout heads first because they are less resistant to damage from freezing and thawing. Heavy frost improves sprouts' taste.

You can store potatoes in the garden by digging a pit eighteen to twenty inches deep. Put the potatoes in the pit and cover them with a plastic sheet large enough to extend past the edges of your pit. Dump leaves over the plastic to form a generous mound. Cover the mound so the leaves stay in place and anchor the cover with stones or boards. Any time you need potatoes, lift the plastic film and help yourself. If, in spite of your protection, the temperature in the pit stays below 45 degrees F. the potatoes will become sweet because their starch will turn to sugar. However, if you keep them at 70 degrees F. for about a week, the sugar will convert back to starch.

Parsnips and Jerusalem artichokes can be left in the ground without protection, to be harvested the following spring.

Properly insulating your garden will protect your crops from temperatures down to minus 20 degrees F.; if the temperature gets colder, your ground will freeze.

You can also plan your garden to provide you with herbs early in the spring. If planted in a corner of the garden protected from winds, the top-multiplier onion (Egyptian onion) and chives will gratify you with early greens. Multiplier onions need room because, as their name suggests, they multiply. They form a cluster of little bulbs at the end of a stem that eventually bends over to the ground to form a new generation of greens.

Parsley planted the previous year appears a little later in the spring. Italian, or plain, parsley is your best bet because it is vigorous and tastes better than other parsley varieties.

CHAPTER 6

Seeds

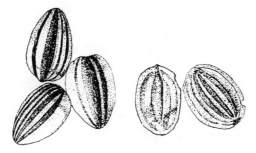

History

Seeds, including vegetable seeds, were on earth long before agriculture was born some 12,000 years ago. Any vegetable that reaches your table has a long history. Wild turnips, radishes, onions, squash, and cabbage were known to prehistoric people who spent a good part of their time foraging for them. We have no proven explanation of how man learned to discriminate between edible and inedible plants. However, we can speculate that hungry humans would investigate all available plants and—through trial and error—discover which ones were edible. Stalking vegetables was easier than stalking game, it just took a while to learn which plants were worth looking for.

Agriculture emerged when humans realized that seeds from useful plants could be planted and the resulting plants harvested. With their food supply under control, humans refined their activities and divisions of labor to give rise to what is now cumulatively known as civilization.

Humans modified the original plants provided by Mother Nature with the advance of civilization. We have evidence that 6,000 years ago the Incas of Central America grew domesticated plants. They even practiced selective breeding of plant species with preferred traits. When the Spaniards invaded the New World in the latter part of the fifteenth century, they found highly improved domestic species of potatoes, tomatoes, corn, and squash.

Our domestic vegetables did not originate in any particular area of the globe. Instead, agriculture began nearly simultaneously in different parts of the world. Then, gradually, our vegetables and fruits journeyed around the globe. People spread plants, seeds, and roots; wind and birds helped, too, carrying seeds great distances.

The Seed Industry

Refining plant varieties has preoccupied humans for thousands of years. Two types of seeds are now available to the gardener: open-pollinated and hybrid. Today, scientific knowledge applied by private, profit-seeking organizations has resulted in the seed industry. Plant breeders hired by private seed companies or land-grant colleges work full-time developing new or improved crop varieties. As an example, in 1979, we witnessed the birth of a new kind of pea, the

Sugar Snap—one welcome result of the competition between seed companies, large and small, to offer new and better varieties.

Plant scientists seek to produce varieties to meet all types of needs. Commercial tomato growers needed a new type of tomato to switch from manual to mechanical harvesting. Through genetic manipulation, plant breeders produced a variety of tomato whose fruit would ripen uniformly, with a tough skin and little juice. These traits facilitated quick, mechanical harvesting.

But that tomato had a problem: it was round, and round tomatoes roll off factory conveyor belts. So scientists returned to the laboratory and emerged with the famous "square" tomato. It also had no flavor, but since it was used solely for processing into paste products, this didn't matter.

Iceberg lettuce is another example of a variety developed for growers. It can be picked mechanically and withstands lengthy shipping. By the time it reaches your table it is still crunchy, still tasteless, and still almost without nutritional value.

Some plant breeders concern themselves with the needs of the home gardener. They are responsible for excellent tasting varieties that you never see in the stores, because these varieties are not profitable for large growers. Home garden varieties are often more fragile and deteriorate quickly during shipment.

Like supermarket produce, most seeds sold through grocery stores are designed for mass marketing, not for your region's specific climate. As a new gardener you might buy varieties that take a long time to mature—too long for the cold climate. You can do far better with varieties selected from a seed company catalog. Consult your county extension agent about what grows best in your area. And if you have access to a nursery that regionalizes its seed selection, you should support it. (See *Varieties for Cold Climates*, page 83, *Seed Companies*, page 133.)

When selecting your seeds pay special attention to the letters AAS, All-American Selection. This seal of approval signifies that the variety is proven to give the best results under different growing conditions.

Finally, as you become a seasoned gardener you will acquire preferences for varieties that work well for you. It is, therefore, disconcerting to see some favorite varieties taken off the market without warning. Even though seed companies often replace them with "new and improved" varieties, you are not ready to change. If your preferred variety is open-pollinated, consider saving your own seeds. But this is not an alternative if you are working with hybrids.

Hybrid Seeds

A hybrid is created by cross pollinating two different varieties of the same plant. The hybrid plant breeder seeks to combine the  desirable characteristics of two parent plants to produce superior offspring: the results sought include better yield, more vigor, and/ or improved resistance to diseases, insects, and extreme temperatures.

The characters "F1" following the name of a vegetable indicate a first generation hybrid. Hybrid seeds should not be saved for replanting. They are not necessarily sterile, but the new plants assume the traits of one of their mother plant's parents and produce vegetables of inconsistent quality.

Hybrid seeds are expensive if it is difficult to imitate a particular plant's propagation methods. For example, plant breeders can easily produce hybrid corn, making these seeds plentiful and inexpensive. But breeders find it difficult to produce hybrid tomatoes.

Don't Always Blame the Seeds

If you are disappointed in the quality of a vegetable you've grown, don't be too hasty to blame the seed or the seed company. Even if you selected the right varieties for your region, you might still end up with poor results.

Varieties do not perform according to description if you give them poor growing conditions. The taste and nutritional value of a vegetable depend on the weather, the soil, the availability of water, and the amount of sun. The same variety of carrots, for example, tastes differently when grown in different soils, or with different exposure to the sun. Most vegetables need at least six to eight hours of sun per day. If your garden lacks that minimal amount, you are asking for inferior produce.

Pay attention to the quality of your soil if you want high quality vegetables. If your soil is healthy with organic matter, you will improve the plant's conversion of solar energy into greenery.

Finally, a word about the difference between most store-bought and home-grown vegetables. You will notice that your cucumbers do not shine like the waxed ones in the store, your celery is not as white, and your carrots vary in shape. As consumers we have been led to believe that consistent, blemish-free appearance equates with good flavor. But we place too much emphasis on cosmetics. Once you eat the first vegetables you have grown yourself, you will learn that cosmetics matter little for superior flavor.

Varieties for Cold Climates

The following list of varieties suitable for cold climates is divided into two sections: Cool-Season Vegetables and Warm-Season Vegetables. As the names suggest, you can plant cool-season vegetables earlier in the season, and they do not fare well during the hot summer months; warm-season vegetables must be planted in warmer soil, and gardeners often start them indoors and transplant them later.

Within each section, following the name of the vegetable, you will usually find specific variety names underlined. Following the name comes a brief description of the variety. Within the parentheses you will find the number of days it takes for the variety to reach maturity. The days to maturity vary between seed catalogs, which can be frustrating. Actually, since maturity days vary in relation to weather and to where the vegetables are grown, you will find the days to maturity to give you only a general idea of when your vegetables will mature.

Also, within parentheses you will find a code telling you which seed companies sell that particular variety, but only those varieties that usually must be ordered from catalogs. If you can generally find a variety locally, no additional information is provided. (Seed companies' mailing addresses can be found in **Appendix I**, page 133.)

For example, under cabbage you will find:

Early Red Cabbage
Lasso—two to four lbs. (70 days-I); *Red Acre*—four lbs. (76 days-C).

Early Red Cabbage is the vegetable; *Lasso* and *Red Acre* are the variety names, followed by the weight of the cabbages they produce; 70 days and 76 days are the days to maturity; and I and C are abbreviations for Johnny's Selected Seeds and Burpee, respectively, the seed companies that carry these varieties.

Here is the code for the seed companies:

A—Abundant Life Seed Foundation

B—Seeds Blum

C—Burpee

D—The Cook's Garden

E—De Giorgi Seed Company

F—Garden City Seeds

G—Gurney

H—High Altitude Gardens

I—Johnny's Selected Seeds

J—Jung Quality Seeds

K—Nichols Garden Nursery

L—Park Seed

M—The Rocky Mountain Seed Company

N—Shepherd's Garden Seeds

O—Southern Exposure Seed Exchange

P—Stokes Seeds, Inc.

Q—Territorial Seeds

Cool-Season Vegetables

ASPARAGUS
Mary Washington, Viking (P).

Always plant this perennial in a permanent location.

Most gardening books tell you to grow asparagus from roots planted deeply in well-built trenches. However, growers developed the trench method for mechanical cultivation and it is not necessary for the home gardener. Although you must spread asparagus roots well when you plant them, a hole or small trench will suffice. Plant the roots six inches deep. You can expect a partial harvest in two years and a full harvest by the third year.

—HINT—
To make cultivation more simple, try to grow your asparagus from seeds—not from roots. As with roots, plant in a permanent bed, then thin until the plants are ten inches apart. You can expect a partial harvest in your third year and a full harvest in the fourth.

BEETS
Early Wonder; Detroit Dark Red—Detroits seem to have a darker color (60 days); *Formanova* (60 days-I); *Cylindra*—instead on being round, these beets are cylindrical and long; they give a higher yield per square foot than other varieties (60 days-C); *Burpee Golden*—excellent flavor and do not bleed when cooked; however, seeds germinate poorly, so plant more per row than the instructions specify (55 days-C); *Lutz Green Leaf Winter Keeper*—this less popular variety is worth trying. The beets grow larger than others but remain sweet, and the greens are excellent when steamed. As the name indicates, these beets store well (80 days-C).

Plant the seeds a half inch deep, and thin the rows when the plants are three to four inches tall. The large seeds should be planted sparingly because each pod contains a group of seeds. Ultimately, space individual plants three to four inches apart.

—HINT—
For a richer taste, bake your beets, individually wrapped in aluminum foil, at 350 degrees F. for an hour.

BROCCOLI

Green Comet Hybrid (55 days-C); *Premium Crop Hybrid* (60 days-P); *Italian Green Sprouting* (70 days); *De Cicco* (60 days-J).

Several reasons lie behind this vegetable's popularity among gardeners. Not only is it nutritious, with large amounts of calcium, iron, and vitamins A and C, but it requires less care than any other member of the cabbage family. And, after producing a central head, broccoli puts out a continuous supply of smaller but equally usable side shoots until the first frost.

Plants should be spaced fifteen to eighteen inches apart.

—HINTS—

Peeled stems of broccoli can substitute for water chestnuts in Chinese dishes.

Raw broccoli has a much higher vitamin content than when cooked. (Three ounces of raw broccoli contain 113 milligrams of Vitamin C, compared to 50 milligrams in a comparable amount of orange juice.)

BRUSSELS SPROUTS

Jade Cross Hybrid (90 days-C); *Early Dwarf Danish* (95 days-H,F); *Long Island Improved* (90 days-K).

Space plants fifteen inches apart. If you want mild taste, don't harvest until after a good frost. Firm sprouts will winter over under a blanket of snow.

—HINTS—

To encourage more vigorous sprouts, snip off the top two inches of the plants in September.

For faster cooking make a crisscross cut a half inch deep at the bottom of each sprout.

CABBAGE

The prince of plants! True, it needs room, but homegrown cabbage tastes far superior to store-bought. You can plant early, mid-season, and late varieties of cabbage at the same time, but they will mature at different rates. The dates on seed packets refer to the maturation time after you transplant seedlings. If you grow cabbage from seed, add at least a month.

Early Cabbage
Earliana—two to four lbs. (60 days-C,E); *Golden Acre*—two to three lbs. (60 days-E,F); *Prima*—two to three lbs. (60 days-I); *Early Jersey Wakefield*—two to three lbs. Cone-shaped head, known for its delicate flavor (63 days-I).

—HINT—
When you cut early cabbage heads, leave the stems in the ground; by fall they will form clusters of small cabbages.

Early Red Cabbage (Early red cabbage stores poorly.)
Lasso—two to four lbs. (70 days-I); *Red Acre*—four lbs. (76 days-C).

Mid-season Cabbage
Copenhagen Market—four lbs. (72 days); *Stonehead*—four lbs. (70 days-P); *Glory of Enkhuizen*—six lbs. (75 days-F).

Late Cabbage
Danish Roundhead—five to seven lbs. (105 days-C); *Late Flat Dutch*—ten lbs. (105 days-G); *Penn. State Ballhead*—eight lbs. (110 days-F); *Brunswick*—six lbs. (85 days-F).

Late Red Cabbage
Mammoth Red Rock—eight to ten lbs. Stores well. (100 days-C).

Savoy Cabbage
Savoy Ace Hybrid—four lbs. (90 days-C); *Blue Max*—four lbs. (78 days-I).
Savoy cabbage withstands heat well and can survive modest fall frosts. Its crinkled leaves discourage cabbage butterflies, which like to lay their eggs on the underside of smooth leaves. It also tastes superior to standard varieties

CHINESE CABBAGE

Chinese cabbage can be difficult to grow because it is sensitive to plentiful summer sunshine and goes to seed easily. But persevere, because this cabbage is a must for real Chinese cooking and is rich in vitamins. You will soon discover how to grow it best in your area. Most gardeners find early spring or fall planting to be more successful.

Napa Cabbage
Nerva Hybrid (46 days-I); *Blues Hybrid* (50 days-I); *Two Seasons Hybrid* (62 days-C); *Orient Express* (43 days-C).
This type forms oval-shaped solid heads, excellent in stir fries and for salads or coleslaw.

Pak Choi Cabbage
Lei-Choi—forms stalks like celery, but white (50 days-C); *Mei Qing Choi*—smaller than *Lei-Choi* and easy to grow (45 days-C); *Tah Tsai*—especially suited for spring and fall planting; this green forms rosettes growing close to the ground, deep green and very nutritious. Add to soups or cook with other vegetables (45 days-K).

CARROTS

Instead of planting your carrots in rows, scatter them in a bed about one-foot wide. This method has two advantages: the plants' roots will grow straight and the carrot patch will require less space. If you do plant in rows, use your seeds sparingly, and place the rows eight to ten inches apart. Some gardeners add sand to carrot seeds to ensure sparse sowing, or you can integrate radish seeds in the same rows; they will mark your rows. You can also sow radishes between rows of carrots; in forty-five days you can harvest the radishes, and the carrots will have plenty of room to grow.

To be sweet, carrots need a sunny spot. All carrots prefer light, healthy soil. Heavy soil produces tough carrots.

Long Carrots
A Plus Hybrid—seventy-six percent higher carotene content (75 days-J); *Gold Pak*—eight to ten inches long (77 days-J).

Half-long Carrots
Danver, Chantenay, Nantes (70 days); *Touchon* (70 days-E); *Scarlet Keeper*—six to seven inches long (85 days-F); *Minicor*—very early carrot (55 days-I).

Short Carrots
Little Finger (65 days-J); *Burpee Short' n Sweet* (68 days-C); *Kinko*—three to four inches long (55 days-I); *Parmex* or *Paris Market*—round, one and a half inches in diameter (50 days-I).
These varieties work well if you have shallow soil.

—HINTS—
Freshly manured soil causes carrots to split or fork as they grow.
You can leave your carrots in the ground during the winter. After the first freeze, cover them with plastic bags tightly stuffed with dry leaves. Later, simply lift a bag and dig out your carrots. This protects adequately down to minus 20 degrees F. In windy locations pile a blanket of loose leaves over the bags, and secure them with a plastic sheet.

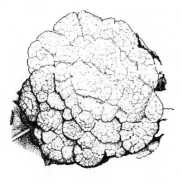

CAULIFLOWER
Cauliflower is more difficult to grow and more susceptible to frost than other members of the cabbage family. To obtain pure white heads on early varieties, pin the outer leaves together after they have become dry over the head with a clothes pin. This keeps sunlight from reaching the head, causing discoloration. If you like small cauliflowers for individual servings, sow seeds directly and space six to eight inches apart. With this method, some varieties perform better than others. Try Andes, Alert, or Dominant.

Early Cauliflower
Snow Crown Hybrid (50 days-I); *Early Snowball* (50 days-P); *Alert* (45 days-P); *Early White Hybrid* (52 days-C).

Mid-season Cauliflower
Dominant (68 days-P); *Andes* (68 days-I); *Self-Blanche* (72 days-J).

Purple Cauliflower
Violet Queen Hybrid (54 days-I, J).
An easy-to-grow combination of cauliflower and broccoli. It does not need any tying.

—HINT—
For a different-tasting cauliflower dish lightly brown one-third cup bread crumbs in a frying pan, add steamed cauliflower flowerets, and stir.

CELERY
Giant Pascal (110 days-M); *Ventura (*80 days-I); *Golden Self-Blanching* (100 days-J).
Don't plant celery seeds directly in your garden; instead, start them indoors about twelve weeks before the suggested planting date. Set transplants about eight inches apart.

Supermarket celery is blanched. This procedure whitens the celery stalk and can be done by several methods. To blanch your celery hill the soil on both sides of the celery row tightly around the stalks. This procedure makes the celery hard to clean but by wrapping paper around the plant, or placing boards secured by pegs on both sides of the row, you can avoid this problem. In any event, absence of light blanches the celery.

However you don't need to blanch your celery. Unblanched celery tastes better and is more nutritious.

Celery needs rich soil and a dependable supply of water; the vegetable itself contains ninety-five percent water.

—HINT—
Slice celery stalks diagonally and cook in very little water for five minutes. They should still be crisp. Pour out the water, add sliced almonds and serve with chicken or pork. You can also stir fry celery. Add the almonds at the last minute.

FRENCH CELERY
Dinant (K).
This celery tastes stronger than normal celery and grows well in cold climates. It produces many narrow stalks, excellent in soups and stews, and it can be dried for winter use. Think of it as an herb. Two or three plants give you all

the fresh celery you need. You don't have to start these seeds indoors; once you can work your soil, simply plant the seeds about a quarter inch deep. This celery is a biennial that winters well without protection. Let it bloom the second year, and it will reseed itself.

FAVA BEANS OR BROAD BEANS
Broad Windsor Long Pod (65 days-P); *Ipro*—smaller pods but tolerant to heat (78 days-I).

If you cannot grow lima beans, these provide acceptable substitutes. In addition, the plants look beautiful in your garden, especially the flowers and the velvety green seed pods. Plants grow up to three feet tall.

Plant two inches deep. Thin to eight inches apart.

—HINT—
Cut down fava beans after spring harvest to induce new growth for a fall crop. Plants are hardy down to 12 degrees F.

GARLIC
Spanish Red (F); *California Early* (O).

Everybody should plant this indestructible, pest-free, and easy-to-grow plant in their garden. In late October plant the cloves from the outside of a garlic bulb four inches deep, and cover with two inches of soil. You can plant in the spring, but your garlic heads will be smaller.

It is fine to plant the garlic you buy at the store, but if you are going to plant garlic, you might as well plant the best tasting and longest-lasting variety. Red garlic meets these standards better than white garlic. A fresh clove of garlic that explodes with juices under the touch of a knife makes the effort of finding and planting a good variety well worthwhile.

Many gardening articles and books talk about elephant garlic. It belongs to a different species than common garlic and takes two seasons to mature. The size of the cloves is impressive, but the mild taste compares poorly with true garlic.

—HINT—
The best dressing for butterhead lettuce is a homemade vinaigrette. Add a minced clove of garlic to your oil and vinegar, and the taste becomes rich.

JERUSALEM ARTICHOKE
Jerusalem Artichoke (G).

This little-known tuber, a member of the sunflower family, deserves more attention than it gets. It is a starchless, low-calorie vegetable ideal for people on low carbohydrate diets. When cooked, the tubers taste like artichokes.

In early spring plant tubers four to five inches deep and ten inches apart. Plant Jerusalem artichokes in a secluded area, because the roots tend to spread, and the plants will invade other parts of your garden. Each plant will grow about eight feet tall and produce about two pounds of tubers. Jerusalem artichokes are virtually indestructible: the tubers can be left in the ground during the winter, even without protective mulch, then harvested at your convenience.

—HINTS—

Jerusalem artichokes provide a quick growing hedge, the perfect screen for your compost pile.

The tubers can substitute for water chestnuts in many recipes.

You can add them raw to salads. Do not peel the tubers; just scrub them.

KALE

Dwarf Blue Curled Vates (55 days-C); *Konserva* (60 days-I); *Red Russian* (60 days-A,Q).

You will find it impossible to grow a bad variety of kale. Kale deserves greater popularity. The hardiest of the cole family, kale grows well even under adverse conditions. In fact, frost improves its flavor. When young, kale can substitute for lettuce.

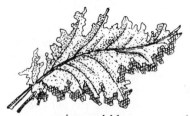

A spring and a summer planting gives you a continuous supply of greens. Kale grows free from pests and is not even susceptible to cabbage worms. You can harvest it throughout the winter. It then starts its new growth in the spring and blooms around May. The flower buds taste like broccoli; the bountiful, green, savoyed leaves, rich in Vitamins A and C, have a flavor somewhere between cabbage and spinach.

Store-bought kale becomes tough and peppery, because it is rarely fresh. But straight from your garden it tastes delightful.

Plant a half inch deep. Thin plants to ten inches apart.

—HINT—

Cook one cup of brown rice until almost tender. Chop a few kale leaves, removing the center ribs. Steam the leaves, mix with the brown rice in a baking dish, dot with margarine, and bake at 350 degrees for 30 minutes. Enjoy a completely new taste.

KOHLRABI
Grand Duke Hybrid (50 days-C); *Early White Vienna* (55 days); *Early Purple Vienna* (60 days).

This vegetable forms an apple-like bulb above the ground. It tastes delicious raw.

You can easily grow kohlrabi from seeds. Plant a half inch deep, and thin the seedlings to six inches apart in rows ten inches apart.

—HINT—
Since kohlrabi bulbs form above the ground, you don't have to worry about root maggots. Kohlrabi provides a good substitute for turnips, which are susceptible to root maggots.

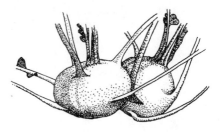

LEEKS
This vegetable belongs in the onion family but does not form a bulb. Instead, it is grown for its stem. Leeks are hardy, easy to grow, ideal for cold climates, and pest free. Leeks do not taste like onions; they are mild, aromatic, and you can use them for soups, stir frying and as a substitute for scallions.

Early Summer Leeks
King Richard (75 days-I); *Varna* (70 days-I).

Plant a half inch deep in the spring in an open area. Thin seedlings to six inches apart.

Bred to grow long stems, these varieties do not need to be hilled—they are a lazy gardener's delight. They keep poorly in the winter.

Late Winter Leeks
Broad London or American Flag (130 days); *Giant Carentan* (120 days-A); *Giant Musselburg* (120 days); *Durabel* (120 days-Q); *Alaska* (105 days-P).

Summer and winter leeks show their differences in their leaves: light green for summer varieties and dark blue-green for winter varieties.

You can start late-leek varieties indoors in February or March, or sow directly outdoors as soon as you can till your soil. Leeks gain vigor through transplanting. Trim the tops and roots of seedlings, and plant in furrows up to the first leaf in order to blanch the stems. During the growing season, hill up soil around the stems with a hoe two or three times. This procedure also encourages the stems to grow taller.

Like summer leeks, winter leeks can be sown directly and will perform well. This means that anyone can grow leeks without fuss.

Leeks keep better during the winter when protected with a mulch of dry leaves.

—HINT—

The famous vichyssoise is not authentic without leeks. For another soup—quick and healthy—boil two cubed potatoes in a quart of beef or chicken stock with a large chopped leek for 30 minutes. Mash with a potato masher and season with salt and pepper.

LETTUCE

Lettuce comes in so many varieties on seed-rack displays in stores and through catalogs that it is impossible not to feel like a kid in a candy store. Let your taste buds be the judge, and see for yourself which varieties you prefer.

Leaf Lettuce

Black Seeded Simpson—the earliest, but not the tastiest (40 days); *Early Prizehead* (45 days); *Green Ice* (45 days-C); *Oak Leaf* (45 days); *Cocarde*— a red oak leaf (46 days-I); *Salad Bowl* (45 days); *Red Salad Bowl* (50 days-C); *Red Sails* (45 days); *Deer Tongue* or *Matchles*—triangular leaves (This variety refuses to bolt, making it perfect for a small garden but not so good if you want to save your own seeds.) (50 days-D,F).

Plant leaf lettuce seeds a half inch deep. Thin seedlings to eight to ten inches apart and use the thinnings for early salads. Also, if you have an empty spot available, transplant some thinnings for a later crop. All leaf lettuces lend themselves to the cut-and-come-again method. If you cut your plants back when they are four to six inches high, you can expect good quality regrowth.

Whatever lettuce you plant, do not make the mistake of planting long rows. Instead plant short rows every two weeks for a continuous supply of prime quality lettuce. Select slow-bolting varieties as you go into summer.

Soil temperatures above 80 degrees F. prevent lettuce seeds from germinating. In hot weather start lettuce in flats, where you can control the temperature, and then transplant.

Iceberg Lettuce

Ithaca (75 days-P); *Salinas* (75 days-Q); *Rosa*—a red iceberg lettuce and easy to grow (80 days-Q); *Great Lakes*—good for hot weather (90 days-C); *Red Grenoble*—a versatile French lettuce. Can be used as a loose-leaf lettuce, but if left to mature, will form heads (55 days-D).

The most common type of head lettuce sold in stores, iceberg lettuce has good shipping qualities and keeps well in storage. As consumers, we have managed to acquire a taste for it. Actually, store-bought lettuce doesn't have much to offer except crunchiness. Yet you can be assured that the iceberg lettuce grown in your garden will have taste.

Leave one foot between plants. Once heads are formed, overhead watering encourages rotting or sliminess. Thus, surface irrigation works best for this type of lettuce.

Cos or Romaine Lettuce

Parris Island (70 days); *Rosalita*—deep-red romaine, more resistant to heat and cold weather (65 days-C); *Winter Density*—compact head, somewhere between a romaine and a bib; practically all the leaves can be used (60 days-I); *Little Gem* or *Sugar Cos* or *Sucrine*—fast-growing with small, tender heart (45 days-H,C,D).

Butterhead or Bibb Lettuce

Bibb—small hearts (55 days); *Buttercrunch*—more heat resistant than Bibb; can be grown successfully all summer and produces larger heads (75 days); *Canada Boston*—good tasting and does not bolt easily (68 days-P); *Merveille des 4 Saisons* (Marvel of Four Seasons)—red-tinged leaves (60 days-C,F); *Canasta* (50 days-I); *Victoria* (52 days-I); *Anenue*—seeds germinate in hot weather (50 days-I); *Nancy* (58 days-I).

Sometimes these varieties require a longer growing period and fit somewhere between loose-leaf and heading lettuces. They all have exceptional texture and taste—a must for gourmet salads—and you can find few of them in grocery stores. The outside leaves protect a cream-colored heart, although virtually the whole plant can be used.

Endive or Fall Lettuce

FEATHERY-LEAFED ENDIVE: *Green Curled* (90 days-C); *Green Curled Ruffec* (90 days-K); *President* (80 days-Q).

BROAD-LEAFED ENDIVE: *Escarole* or *Broad-leafed Batavian* (90 days).

This type of lettuce is hard to find in seed catalogs because it is not always listed under the heading of lettuce. Seed companies instead list it alphabetically, or under "salad greens." Endive can be added to salads or used as a complete salad in itself. It tastes slightly bitter, with a tougher texture than regular lettuce. Intolerant to heat, endive tolerates cold well and thus is an ideal late season lettuce, especially with some protection.

You can grow two types of endives: feathery-leafed and broad-leafed.

You can use the blanched hearts of both kinds of endive in salads and the outer leaves for garnish. For fuller hearts blanch the endives by circling the head with a large rubber band. To prevent rotting, do not use overhead watering. This lettuce is worth growing and deserves your acquiring a taste for it. If you provide it with some protection, you can enjoy this lettuce up to Christmas time and beyond.

Corn Salad or Mache

Corn Salad (60 days-P,I).

This indestructible oddity grows wild in some parts of Europe and merits more acceptance among gardeners than it has had. Its size is not impressive; it forms small dark rosettes with a pungent taste. You can add corn salad to larger salads or use it alone for a gourmet salad with lots of vitamins. Leave a plant or two to go to seed and it will reseed itself. For a continuous supply, plant in the spring and again in August for a fall crop. It overwinters, even under harsh conditions.

Chicory

GREEN CHICORY: *Sugarhat* or *Sugar Loaf* or *Sugar Hat*—has a tight conical head that resembles romaine lettuce. It refuses to bolt and remains intact even after severe frosts; tastes delicious in a tossed salad, or braised (70 days-K); *Magdeburgh* or *Cicoria Siciliana*—can be used for its greens, but try harvesting the roots in the fall, and then dry and roast them for a coffee substitute (100 days-P); *Catalogna* or *Radichetta*—can be harvested very young or at the adult stage (40 days-I); *Belgian Endive* or *Witloof* (120 days-C); *Toner Hybrid*—Witloof and Toner were developed for forcing and grown solely for their roots. Plant seeds in the spring and collect the parsnip-like roots in the fall. Force the plants in a cool, dark area following the instructions included with the order or packet. When forced, the roots produce a growth of tight, creamy, elongated heads called "chicons." You can grow this otherwise expensive salad in the middle of the winter (130 days-I)

RED CHICORY (RADICCHIO): Red chicory should be planted at different times according to the climate. Chicory likes a chilling growing period to give good results.

Giulio—can be planted early in the spring and will successfully produce large heads (60 days-I); *Augusto* (70 days-I); *Adria*—can be planted early in the spring and will successfully produce large heads (75 days-P); *Rouge de Verona*—will respond better if planted for a fall crop and will overwinter for an early crop the following spring (85 days-K).

Although seed catalogs do not include chicory in the lettuce sections, it should be considered a kissing cousin to lettuce.

All types of chicory are disease free.

Mesclun

Mesclun (45 days-D).

The latest rage in lettuce, mesclun is a mix of greens and herbs selected for flavor, and then mixed to create a tantalizing blend. Today, mesclun appears to be novel, but the immigrants of 300 years ago knew it well.

Mesclun is harvested with the cut-and-come-again method, and, consequently, all the plants included in this mix have similar growing patterns. Seed packets usually list the plants included in the mix, and the relative numbers vary between seed companies. The standard mix contains varieties of loose-leaf lettuce, chicory, and herbs like chervil, cress, and arugula. Nothing in the seed company mixes prevents you from preparing your own custom-made mixture.

Sow a quarter inch deep in a bed or in rows four to six inches apart. Make continuous plantings.

MUSTARD GREENS

Tendergreens (35 days); *Green Wave* (45 days-I); *Kyona* or *Mizuna*—a Japanese variety that forms a bushy plant with fringed leaves; mild in taste and resistant to heat (40 days-K,Q); *Tyfon Holland Greens* (40 days-K); *Arugula* — its piquant flavor becomes too peppery in hot weather; use only young, tender leaves (40 days).

This fast-growing vegetable does well only in cool weather.

You can plant your rows as little as eight inches apart and then, once they're harvested, use the space for something else. The greens are rich in vitamins A and C. Plants do not have to be pulled for harvesting, instead the leaves can be pinched, and new growth will continue.

ONIONS

Early Yellow Globe (100 days-I); *New York Early* (98 days-P); *Southport Red Globe* (100 days-P); *White Sweet Spanish* (120 days-C,P)—these varieties all keep well. *Early Yellow Sweet*—doesn't keep well but has excellent taste (100 days-Q).

You can grow onions from seeds, sets, or plants. The advantage of using seeds is that you can choose the variety you desire. Sets or plants produce more quickly, but seed companies generally sell them by color—white or yellow—without reference to the specific variety. Occasionally seed companies indicate the variety of the plant or set.

Individual onion sets should be marble-sized or smaller, about 200 sets per pound. Don't buy from any company that sells big sets, because you get fewer sets per pound.

Onions prefer well-drained soil and plenty of sunshine. They need a daily dose of about twelve hours of sun to mature fully.

If you use sets, place them close together so you can harvest scallions when you thin your rows. Thin the plants to five to six inches apart.

—HINT—
You will find globe onions easier to peel. You don't have to fight the indentation of the flat varieties that you so often get with sets.

Top Multiplier or Egyptian Onion
Top Multiplier or *Egyptian Onion* (O).

You can leave this variety in the ground all year. Early in the spring it produces green onions similar to scallions; however, later in the season you might find the flavor too strong. The top multiplier propagates itself by forming a cluster of bulbs at the end of a stalk. The weight of those little bulbs bends the stem, so the bulbs can touch the ground and take root.

Shallots
Shallots (I,C).

Shallots belong to the onion family, and some grocery stores sell them at a high price. For good reason people value them for gourmet cooking—they taste wonderful.

Plant one shallot in the spring and you will harvest a cluster of ten or twelve in the fall. Most gardeners prefer the red shallot. You don't need to order them from a mail-order seed catalog, since you can plant the shallots you buy in the market.

Press each bulb five inches apart into the well prepared soil, and make sure the top is not completely buried. Not only do shallots grow well in cold climates, they also keep well.

Bunching Onions or Scallions
Evergreen Hardy White (65 days-I).

Scallions are hardy and overwinter easily.

PARSLEY
Plain Dark Green Italian (78 days); *Moss Curled* (80 days)

The plain parsley has a far superior flavor, grows up to twenty-four inches tall, and is very productive. Don't plant too much.

Plant in a well-drained area, and your parsley will return the next year. Parsley is biennial; let one plant go to seed after the second year, and you will have a permanent bed. Parsley withstands light frost and endures heat.

Plant a quarter inch deep. It takes three weeks to germinate. Thin seedlings to six inches apart.

—HINT—
Parsley is high in chlorophyll and makes an excellent mouth freshener—just chew a sprig.

PARSNIP
Hollow Crown (105 days-C); *Harris Early Model* (120 days-J); *Fullback Short Thick* (95 days-J).

This long-rooted vegetable needs good, deep soil. Normal roots grow about a foot in length, except for Fullback, with roots five to eight inches long and better suited for heavy or shallow soil.

Although parsnips can be harvested in the fall, a good frost greatly enhances their flavor.

Plant a half inch deep. Thin seedlings to six inches apart.

—HINT—
Parsnips make a good, and interesting, substitute for mashed potatoes.

PEAS

Homegrown peas always taste better than store-bought, but you should pick them at their prime and as close to meal time as possible; the sugar content rapidly turns into starch after harvest.

Peas can be divided into three categories, according to their height.

DWARF PEAS (Eighteen to twenty-four inches tall): *Little Marvel* (60 days); *Progress no. 9* (62 days-J); *Maestro* (61 days-C); *Knight* (56 days-I); *Improved Laxton's Progress* (55 days-P); *Patriot* (58 days-P).

These extra early varieties need little or no support; a few dry branches planted with the peas will suffice.

INTERMEDIATE PEAS (two to three feet tall): *Green Arrow* (70 days-C); *Lincoln* 65 days-P); *Wando*—heat resistant and productive, even when planted late (68 days-C,H); *Grenadier* (70 days-M).

These varieties need support; chicken wire or twigs work well. The peas produce more if you plant them in double rows, three inches apart, with the plants two inches apart. Space each pair of rows two feet apart, with a row of spinach or radishes in between. You can then harvest these fast-growing vegetables before the peas grow too tall.

TALL PEAS (four to six feet tall): *Tall Telephone* or *Alderman* (70 days-P).

The whole row will topple over without dependable support. This variety saves space if you have a high wire fence. Put supports in place when you plant.

Plant one and a half inches deep.

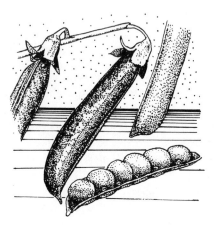

—HINT—

Select varieties resistant to powdery mildew and fusarium wilt. After your peas stop producing, turn them under to bolster your soil with organic matter and the nitrogen that has collected in the little nodules on the peas' roots.

Edible Pod Peas
Edible-podded peas, or Chinese peas, don't have to be shelled; you eat them pods and all. Pick them early before the peas form in the pods. Compared with regular peas, which yield over a short time, the Chinese peas yield generously over a long period—if you keep picking them. Chinese peas taste best steamed or stir-fried, and they freeze well. Seed companies divide edible peas into three categories, according to their height.

DWARF PEAS (sixteen to eighteen inches tall): *Snowbird* (58 days-C); *A Little Sweeties* (60 days-P).
These short plants fool you by producing amazing amounts of pods. They make perfect flowering borders where space is limited.

INTERMEDIATE PEAS (three feet tall): *Oregon Sugar Pod* (68 days-C,G); *Snowflake* (62 days-I); *Dwarf Gray Sugar* (57 days-G).
The plants produce small, but abundant, pods.

TALL PEAS (four to five feet tall): *Mammoth Melting Sugar* (68 days-G).
This tall variety produces pods with a meaty texture. Don't expect abundance.

Snap Peas
Each year, seed companies advertise new vegetables and new varieties, always emphasizing the word "improved." Sometimes the truth differs from the promotion. But when the Sugar Snap was introduced in 1979, the promotional praise was an understatement. This pea combines the best qualities of a Chinese pea and a regular pea, with outstanding sweetness and crispness.

Sugar Snaps do have one drawback: they taste so sweet that they rarely make it from the garden to the table. You'll find it difficult to avoid eating them as you pick.

INTERMEDIATE (two to three feet tall): *Sugar Ann* (60 days-I,P); *Sugar Daddy* (65 days-P); *Sugar Mel*—long pod (70 days-N).

TALL (six feet tall): *Sugar Snap*—very sweet pods (70 days).

—HINT—
Besides eating Sugar Snaps raw (or with a dip) you can steam or stir-fry them. They also freeze well.

POTATOES

If you do not have certified potato sets, make sure you have a reliable source. Bad seed potatoes dash your pre-harvest expectations and make your hard work meaningless.

 A set is simply a small potato or a piece of a large potato. In either case, a set should have two to three eyes and weigh two or three ounces. A potato the size of an egg, with a couple of eyes, makes an excellent set.

Some commercial sets include only one eye and a small amount of flesh. These sets fail to provide enough nourishment to ensure proper germination and produce strong plants. If you order through a seed catalog, look for tubers rather than eyes.

Selecting a potato variety depends on how you like to eat your potatoes. You can get red, yellow, and even blue or purple potatoes, for baking, for salads, for boiling. You can grow early, midseason or late potatoes.

EARLY: Expect new potatoes in July. *Red Norland* (G); *Irish Cobbler*—white (G); *Viking*—red (G).

MIDSEASON: *Norgold Russet*—white (G); *Red Pontiac, Kennebec*—white; *Yukon Gold*—yellow (B); *Yellow Finn*—rich flavor (B); *Desiree*—red skin and yellow flesh (I); *Caribe*—purple (A).

LATE: *Russet Burbank* or *Netted Gem* or *Idaho Russet, Sangre*—red (F); *Bintje*—yellow (B); *Yellow Fingerling*—excellent for salads (B); *Butte*—white; has twenty percent more protein, shallow eyes, and is the perfect size for a medium appetite (G).

Before ordering check with local nurseries to see what is available.

Plant each set five to six inches deep and ten to twelve inches apart, in rows no more than twenty inches apart. Or, if you plant intensively, plant your sets eight to twelve inches apart at equal distances.

You can choose one of several ways of planting your potatoes. Try puting your sets directly on the ground. Cover with hay, straw, or grass clippings. After the potatoes have emerged, keep adding mulch, and be careful to not expose the potato tubers to sunlight. This system has an important advantage: when you want to pick new potatoes, simply reach under the mulch and gather what you need without disturbing the plant.

A variation of this planting technique consists of placing the potato sets on three to five inches of slightly decomposed leaves, an acidic growing medium. (Potatoes like acid soil.) Cover the sets with the mulch of your choice.

If you don't have enough room for potatoes and you have garden paths, you can still have the luxury of new potatoes. Place two to three sets in the path and cover with mulch; you can easily step over the sets while tending the rest of the garden.

Don't worry if your potato plants don't bloom. They will form tubers anyway. If you want to prevent scabby potatoes don't use fresh manure. Aged manure is safe.

—HINTS—

Don't use potatoes from the grocery store as sets; they usually have been treated to prevent sprouting, and this is exactly what you don't want.

Ten pounds of seed potatoes will produce approximately one bushel or sixty pounds.

Potatoes are not fattening; they are low in calories and rich in vitamins and potassium. What you put on the potato—the butter and sour cream—makes the difference.

RADISHES

Eighteen Day—very early (18 days-D); *Cherry Belle* (25 days); *Crimson Giant* (30 days); *French Breakfast* (25 days); *Champion* (25 days); *Sparkler* (25 days); *Comet* (25 days); *Parat German Giant*—amazing; not only does it grow as large as a golf ball, but it will stay firm (30 days-G); *White Icycle* (30 days).

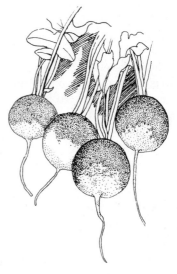

Radish seeds germinate in three days, making them the perfect vegetable for the anxious gardener. They do well only in cool weather and need plenty of water. Try planting in the fall.

If planted alone, radishes can be grown in rows six inches apart or less. Otherwise, they can be planted between rows of slow-germinating vegetables like carrots or parsnips.

Plant a half inch deep. Shortly after they emerge, thin to two inches apart, three inches for the giant varieties. Without thinning, radishes will not form a bulb.

—HINTS—
Discourage root maggots by sprinkling sand, wood ashes, or diatomaceous earth in the rows before planting the seeds. Fall planting also makes radishes less susceptible to root maggots.

Slit your radishes, and fill them with peanut butter. This makes an excellent appetizer.

Winter Radishes
Chinese Rose; Chinese White (55 days)

Winter radishes have large, long roots and, as the names indicate, they are either rose or white. Perhaps because people's habits change slowly, the winter radish has remained less popular among gardeners than the regular radish. But winter radishes are worth checking into.

Because of their longer growing time, winter radishes can fall victim to root maggots.

Plant one half inch deep. Thin seedlings to six inches apart.

RUTABAGAS
Laurentian (95 days-I); *American Purple Top* (90 days); *Altasweet* (92 days-P).

Rutabagas are easily grown, and they keep well. They grow large, up to two pounds, and only rarely become woody.

Plant a half inch deep. Thin seedlings to ten inches apart. To combat root maggots, use the same techniques as you would for radishes.

—HINT—
Peel a rutabaga and slice lengthwise as if for French fries. Cook for twenty minutes in a small amount of water with a sprinkling of thyme. This makes a wonderful vegetable to serve with chicken or pork.

SALSIFY OR OYSTER PLANT
Mammoth Sandwich Island (115 days-P).

Don't get discouraged by this slow grower. You can leave this pest-free vegetable in the ground over the winter. It needs light soil to form its eight-inch long, smooth roots. The flavor, somewhat like oyster, is tantalizing. Plant one half inch deep. Thin seedlings to four inches apart.

—HINTS—
Boil the cut-up salsify first and braise in butter.

Roots left in the ground will grow young shoots you can use for an interesting salad.

SORREL

Sorrel (60 days-I,B).

Wild sorrel grows prolifically along certain roadsides. A patch of cultivated sorrel is far superior for gardens than wild sorrel. Sorrel looks a bit like spinach, with light-green, acidic-tasting leaves.

Sorrel is a perennial and should be given a corner of its own in the garden. Plant a quarter inch deep and thin seedlings to ten inches apart. For a continuous supply of leaves, trim off any flowering stalks.

—HINT—
Add a cupful of chopped leaves to potato soup for a gourmet treat.

SPINACH

Melody Hybrid (42 days-C); *Tyee Hybrid* (42 days-I); *Bloomsdale Long Standing* (42 days).

Plant spinach early because it bolts easily during long summer days. One of the earliest vegetables you can harvest, it confirms the arrival of spring for the gardener.

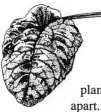

Spinach needs rich soil. If you like to experiment, plant some seeds in the fall, protect with Reemay, and you will have early spinach the next spring. You can also plant in August, and shade it from direct sun for a fall crop.

Plant a half inch deep. Spinach seeds are large, so plant sparingly. Thin seedlings to four to five inches apart.

Spinach contains iron and calcium, but these minerals are locked up in oxalic acid. This acid is responsible for the plant's relatively low nutritional value but also gives it a distinctive taste.

Spinach Substitutes

New Zealand Spinach—a bushy plant, thrives in hot weather (70 days); *Green Orach* (37 days); *Red Orach*—grows tall and as vigorously as a weed. Will reseed itself (37 days-F).

You will find it impossible to grow spinach in the summer, because it bolts so easily, but good substitutes are available. They all have a spinach flavor when cooked. Keep pinching the leaves for a continuous supply.

Plant one inch deep and thin seedlings to ten to twelve inches apart.

Since they don't contain oxalic acid, New Zealand and Orach are more nutritious than regular spinach.

SWISS CHARD
Fordhook Giant (50 days); *Rhubard Chard* (59 days-I).
You can also substitute this green for spinach. It withstands heat better than spinach and has a more mild flavor.
A short row produces all summer. Cut the outside leaves and new leaves will grow back. The plant grows up to two feet tall.
Plant one inch deep. Swiss chard has a beet-like seed that contains more than one germ, so plant the seeds sparsely. Thin seedlings to ten inches apart.

—HINT—
Swiss chard leaves have a large middle rib. You can cook these separately like asparagus.

TURNIPS
Purple Top White Globe (50 days).
This fast-growing vegetable does better as a spring or fall crop than as a summer crop. Unfortunately, turnips are highly susceptible to root maggots. Use the same prevention techniques as with radishes and rutabagas. When planted as a fall crop turnips are practically free of root maggots.
Plant a half inch deep. Thin seedlings to six inches apart.

Warm-Season Fruits and Vegetables

All warm-weather fruits and vegetables are sensitive to cool soil. If the soil temperature falls much below 60 degrees F., the seeds will actually rot before they germinate.

Black plastic overlying your plot helps encourage early germination and plant growth by soaking up sunshine and warming the soil. After you prepare your soil, place black plastic over the area you will plant, and secure the edges with soil. Make crisscross slits for access to the areas where you intend to place your seeds or plants. The black plastic helps keep the soil warmer at night and minimizes fluctuations in soil temperature. Be sure to form an indentation around your seeds or plants to help collect moisture.

If you do not use black plastic, waiting for the soil to warm up in regions with short growing seasons can be frustrating. But you have another way! You can pre-sprout your seeds.

Find a plate or a styrofoam tray such as the kind you buy meat in. Place a sheet of paper towel on it, scatter the seeds loosely (overcrowding is disastrous because the roots of the sprouted seeds become horribly tangled), cover the scattered seeds with another sheet of paper towel, and dampen the towels. Slide the plate or tray into a plastic bag, and tie or tuck under the open edge. Put the whole arrangement in a warm spot, such as on top of a refrigerator.

The seeds germinate in just a few days, and leaving the new little plants in that environment too long results in a tangle of roots. When the roots develop and the first leaves are about to appear, transplant the seedlings outdoors. Take hold of the stem—avoid bruising it—and pull gently. Then transplant to a permanent location. In addition, you can protect seedlings with a row cover like Reemay or a mobile cold frame, accelerating their growth and the warming of the soil.

This method works for beans, corn, squash, and cucumbers. It allows you to plant when the soil temperature is hostile to germination, and it circumvents certain insect and disease problems.

BEANS

Pole Beans

Kentucky Wonder—seven- to eight-inch long, oval pods; pick young before the beans become stringy (70 days); *Blue Lake*—six- to seven-inch long, round pods (60 days); *Romano* or *Italian Pole*—five- to six-inch long, flat, wide pods (60 days); *Burpee Golden*—five- to six-inch long, flat, wide yellow pods (60 days-C); *Fortex*—outstanding twelve-inch long, round pods (60 days-I).

Pole beans yield heavily and give a large return for the space they take. Many gardeners agree that the flavor of pole beans is superior to bush beans. But pole beans require special attention because their vines climb up to eight feet. They need support.

The sophistication of the support is up to you. You can use rough poles planted one foot deep and two feet apart. Holes are easier to make with the help of a crowbar. Or, if you prefer, you can set three poles in a tepee style instead of planting in a row.

Before planting your beans remove one shovelful of dirt by each pole and fill the hole with a mixture of soil and compost. Place six to eight seeds per hole, one inch deep, and thin to the four strongest plants. If you use a trellis or a fence, thin the bean plants to six inches apart.

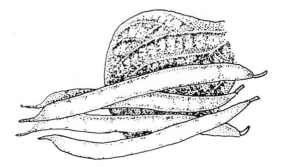

Bush Beans

GREEN BUSH BEANS: *Blue Lake* (55 days); *Improved Tendergreen* (45 days); *Greensleeves* (55 days-C); *Venture* (50 days-I); *Greencrop* (50 days-P); *Early Contender*—all round pods (50 days-G); *Jumbo*—flat, long pods with a strong beany taste (55 days-I); *Romano*—flat, five- to six-inch pods with a strong beany taste (55 days-P).

YELLOW BUSH BEANS: *Pencil Pod Black Wax* (54 days); *Sungold* (47 days-P); *Rocdor* (54 days-I); *Cherokee Wax*—round yellow pods (50 days-G).

Growing pole beans can be cumbersome, which is why gardeners often settle for bush beans; and they come earlier.

With a hoe, make a furrow two inches deep and space the beans two to three inches apart. Thin seedlings to four to six inches apart. You can also plant the seeds in groups of four or five, then space the groups twelve inches apart. If you have room, make another planting three weeks after the first one for a continuous supply of harvestable beans.

—HINTS—
For freezing, use extra green varieties.

Continuous picking encourages all varieties of beans to yield longer.

Lima Beans

Eastland (70 days-P); *Geneva* (85 days-I).

Growing lima beans in cold climates is a challenge, but feasible.

When prolific, lima beans—and bush beans—produce pods that touch the ground, making them susceptible to rot. Prevent this problem by placing a half cylinder made of six-inch mesh or less, concrete-reinforcing wire over the rows. Beans love this type of support, and their pods grow above the wire, which makes picking easy.

—HINT—
If you have a surplus crop of beans, you can use them as green shelled beans or dried beans.

SWEET CORN

The home gardener judges corn by its flavor, sweetness, tenderness, and, in a cold climate, its earliness. The list of varieties to choose from is long and confusing. Corn varieties fall into several categories: standard hybrid, sugar-enhanced, everlasting heritage, xtra-sweet, and open pollinated.

The ears of a standard hybrid sweet corn tend to mature all at the same time and have to be eaten as soon as possible after being picked. Otherwise their sugar converts into starch, and they lose their sweet taste. The SE (sugar enhanced) and EH (everlasting heritage) types have tender kernels and keep their sweetness up to two weeks after maturity.

Corn varieties that belong to the xtra-sweet type indeed taste sweet, and they stay sweet after harvest. However, this corn cannot be planted next to another variety, or they will cross-pollinate, causing the kernels to become starchy and tough. They also germinate poorly in cool soil.

The ears of an open-pollinated corn variety do not mature all at the same time. This type produces ears that are less tender and sweet than hybrid varieties, but some gardeners prefer its flavor.

Plant seeds as close as eight inches apart, in rows a foot apart. Be sure your soil is rich. To guarantee good results, during the growing season add a side-dressing of manure or another nitrogen-rich fertilizer. As your corn grows, the leaves should be dark green; a yellowish color indicates a lack of nitrogen.

Barrel planting yields twice as many cobs as does the standard method. Make a circle two feet in diameter and plant your corn eight inches apart, putting a total of nine plants in the area. Space the circles one foot apart. Plant the seeds one and a half inches deep.

For continuous harvest, select varieties that reach maturity at different times, or plant the same variety at two-week intervals.

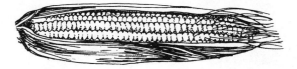

Extra-Early Hybrid Corn

Polar Vee (53 days-P); *Earlivee* (55 days-P); *Buttervee* (58 days-P).

These varieties will surprise you with good-sized cobs on mere three foot stalks. The ears measure six to seven inches long.

Early Hybrid Corn

Seneca Horizon (62 days-P); *Early Sunglow* (63 days-C); *Yukon* (73 days-P).

These varieties grow five feet tall, with seven- to eight-inch long cobs.

Hybrid SE and EH Corn

Sugar Buns (65 days-P); *Precocious* (56 days-P); *Breeder's Choice* (65 days-C); *Kandy Korn EH* (90 days-C); *Platinum Lady*—white kernels (70 days-C).

These varieties grow five to seven feet tall, with seven- to eight-inch long cobs.

Xtra-Sweet Corn

Early Xtra-Sweet (71 days-C); *How Sweet It Is*—white kernels (78 days-C).

Varieties are six to seven feet tall, with eight-inch long cobs.

Open-Pollinated Corn

Golden Bantam (78 days); *Ashworth* (69 days-I).

If you are unfamiliar with open-pollinated varieties, try a small plot and check them out for yourself.

To ensure proper pollination, plant corn in blocks, not single rows. Poor pollination causes empty spots on your cobs. With this in mind, plant two to four consecutive rows of each variety. Don't forget to plant the taller varieties on the north side of the path to prevent shading the shorter varieties.

—HINTS—

Suckers at the base of your corn plants need not be pulled, especially on early varieties. When the corn reaches about a foot in height, plant a few pole beans around the corn patch (except on the north side). The beans will climb the stalks. Or, you can plant cucumbers in the same fashion; their vines thrive in the shade of the corn patch.

CUCUMBERS

PICKLING: *Northern Pickling* (50 days-P); *Liberty Hybrid* (45 days-C); *Pioneer* (51 days-P); *National Pickling* (54 days).

SLICING: *Straight Eight* (52 days); *Marketmore 80* (65 days-I); *Spacemaker*—short vines (54 days-I).

What makes pickling and slicing cucumbers different? The pickling varieties are short and blunt, and the slicing varieties are long. But you can use the pickling varieties for slicing, and vice versa. As a matter of fact, picklers have a softer skin and many gardeners think they taste superior.

Plant seeds one inch deep in rows or hills. Thin to six inches apart in rows, or keep the best three plants in each hill. Space hills three feet apart. Planting in hills does not require you to actually build a mound. The term "hill" refers to a group of seeds planted together.

Cucumbers like to sprawl, but you can save space by encouraging them to grow around a cage two to three feet in diameter made out of six-inch mesh, concrete-reinforcing wire. Plant seeds around the cage and thin the seedlings to six inches apart.

Long Cucumbers

Japanese Long Pickling or *Suyo Long* (65 days-P); *China* (75 days-P).

These varieties deserve particular attention. By far the tastiest cucumbers you can grow, the fruits are long and slender with small seeds and crisp flesh. This type of cucumber should not be peeled and they are burpless. Because the fruits reach at least twelve inches in length, grow them on a trellis or fence to encourage straight fruits.

Bush Cucumbers (See *Varieties for a Small Garden*, page 121.)

—HINTS—

If you have problems with diseases in your area, be sure to select resistant varieties.

Overhead watering encourages diseases in your cucumber patch.

A variety described as "genoecious" bears only female flowers and produces many cucumbers.

EGGPLANT

Dusky Hybrid (60 days-P); *Early Beauty Hybrid* (65 days-C); *Early Black Egg* (65 days-Q,F).

You must start eggplants indoors, eight weeks before transplanting them outdoors. Prepare a spot for each plant by removing a shovelful of soil and replacing it with compost, well-rotted manure, or soil that you have mixed with organic fertilizer. An additional tablespoon of bone meal provides a long-term rich nutrient.

Eggplants are tropical and need warm temperatures. Cover them with Reemay or Agronet to boost the air temperature surrounding the plants and to protect them from flea beetles. Be sure to remove the cover at blooming time. Set the plants twelve to fifteen inches apart.

Eggplants have beautiful purple flowers, making them an attractive addition to a garden.

Oriental Eggplants

Tycoon Hybrid (60 days-K); *Oriental Express Hybrid* (58 days-I).

Oriental varieties prosper in cold climates with cool nights. You can usually harvest by the end of July or early August. They produce long and slender fruits with outstanding texture and taste.

—HINTS—

Here's a simple recipe for Ratatouille, a vegetable casserole well worth trying:

Vegetables needed:
- 2 large onions, sliced
- 2 garlic cloves, minced
- 4 sweet peppers, cut up
- 1 lb. zucchini, cubed
- 1 medium sized eggplant, peeled or unpeeled and cubed
- 4 tomatoes, peeled, seeded and cut up
- salt and pepper to taste
- herbs (chives, parsley, basil)

In a frying pan saute each vegetable separately in olive oil, except the tomatoes. Place the sauted vegetables together in a casserole dish, and add the tomatoes. Season. Cook about thrity minutes. Add the chopped herbs at the end. Serves four.

Ratatouille is good warm or cold. If you have any left over, use it as a filling in an omelet.

Or maybe you'd like some mock caviar? You can make one version of a Middle Eastern dish, Baba Ghanoush, by baking one pound of eggplant at 350 degrees F. until soft. Peel off the skin. Cut up a medium-sized onion and place it in the blender with the eggplant pulp. With the blender or food processor running, gradually add about one cup of oil, a half cup of vinegar, and salt and pepper. Blend until the mixture has the consistency of mayonnaise. This makes a good spread or dip.

MUSKMELONS

REGULAR-SIZED MELONS: *Alaska Hybrid* (70 days-G); *Sweet Granite* (70 days-I); *Burpee Hybrid* (72 days-C,P); *Flyer Hybrid* (68 days-I).

SMALL-SIZED MELONS: *Minnesota Midget* (65 days-G); *Sweet 'N Early Hybrid* (75 days-C,J). These varieties need little space. Their small fruits—about four inches in diameter—are the perfect size for individual servings and ripen well in cold climates.

Melons need consistently warm temperatures. You can start them indoors in peat pots, three seeds per pot, about one month before setting them outside. When transplanting, place the pots two feet apart without disrupting the roots. This is vital: cover with Reemay until the plants become well established. If you have a long enough growing season, you will get better results by planting the seeds directly in the garden when the soil has warmed up. Using black plastic improves the growth.

OKRA

Annie Oakley Hybrid (50 days-I); *Burgundy* (60 days-J); *Perkins Mammoth Long Pod* (50 days-P).

Okra needs sunny days and warm nights to develop fully. Start seeds indoors, one month before the last expected frost. This southern vegetable can be grown in cold climates if you choose the right variety and don't expect too much.

—HINT—

Pick the pods as soon as they reach three inches in length for a continuous yield.

Okra tastes delightful when stir-fried.

SWEET PEPPERS

Start seeds eight to ten weeks before transplanting time. Use the planting procedure recommended for eggplants; however, you can set the peppers closer together than eggplants, eight to ten inches apart.

Bell Peppers

Staddon's Select (70 days-H,B,P); *Early Niagara Giant* (65 days-F,P); *King of the North* (65 days-G); *Jupiter* (70 days-P); *Earliest Red Sweet* (55 days-P); *North Star* (70 days-P); *Ace Hybrid* (60 days-C,P,I)..

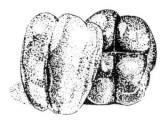 TAPERED FRUIT: *Gypsy Hybrid*—deserves a special chapter. In short, it answers the cold climate gardener's prayers. The plant produces abundantly under the most adverse conditions. The fruits have unequaled flavor (65 days-C,G); *Cubanelle* (68 days-P,B); *Italia* (55 days-I); *Sweet Banana* (60 days); *Lipstick* (55 days-I); *Giant Szegedi* (70 days-P); *Golden Summer*—yellow peppers (70 days-I).

Hot Peppers

Long Red Cayenne (70 days); *Early Jalapeno* (70 days-I); *Hungarian Hot Wax*—dependable and prolific (58 days-I,P); *Tam Jalapeno*—mildly hot (70 days-K); *Mexibell*—a hot bell pepper (60 days-I,K); *Anaheim TMR 23*—although listed with hot peppers, Anaheim should be a category of its own. The plant is tall, reaching twenty-four inches, and produces a large number of long pendant fruits used in chile rellenos. It tastes mild compared with other hot peppers (75 days-C,K).

—HINTS—

All peppers turn red with maturity, but not all become hot; sweet peppers increase in sweetness and vitamin content.

Hot peppers taste hotter around the shoulder; you can control the degree of hotness by removing or leaving the seeds and membranes inside the peppers.

You can easily dry hot peppers for winter use.

You can freeze green peppers without blanching them.

SUMMER SQUASH

GREEN: *Dark Green Zucchini* (50 days); *Greyzini* (50 days-P,M).

YELLOW: *Gold Rush Hybrid*—like zucchini, but yellow (50 days- I,P); *Early Crookneck* 53 days); *Seneca Prolific* (50 days-P).

Zucchini-type summer squash produces prolifically. Two hills will amply supply an average family. Place five or six seeds in each hill. Space the hills three feet apart. Plant the seeds one inch deep. Thin to the best three plants.

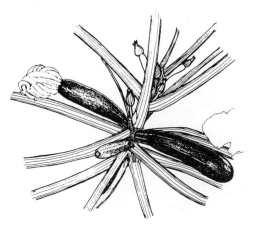

Summer Scallop Squash

White Patty Pan—bland, but when added to other vegetables like tomatoes, peppers, and eggplants, it absorbs their flavors without losing its firmness. You can almost mistake it for mushrooms (54 days); *Peter Pan Hybrid*— light green (50 days-L); *Scallopini*—green (50 days-P); *Sunburst Hybrid*— a piece of art; yellow with a green middle (52 days-I).

Harvest summer scallop squash when it's young—four inches in diameter—for good, delicate flavor. The fruits of scallop squash are round, with scalloped edges.

Since the plants do not sprawl, you can set the hills closer to each other than with other summer squash.

115

Fried zucchini flowers make a delicate appetizer. Coat them with a batter and deep fry them; for a richer taste you can insert a piece of your favorite cheese inside the flowers before dunking them in the batter. Use only the male flowers. Some seed catalogs list a variety called *Butterblossom*, which produce extra male flowers. Actually, all zucchini-type squash produce enough male blossoms, and you can pick them without curbing the fertilization of the female flowers.

WINTER SQUASH

Waltham Butternut—four to five lbs. (90 days-C); *Buttercup* (Burgess Strain)—five lbs. (95 days-P); *Jersey Golden Acorn*—compact plants (80 days-P); *Baby Blue Hubbard*—five to six lbs. (100 days-P); *Sweet Meat* (115 days-Q).

With its high vitamin A content, squash is a valuable winter vegetable. Regular winter squash takes a long time to develop and needs a large area to sprawl. Plant in hills six feet apart.

Planting squash in a corn patch kills two birds with one stone. After you harvest the corn, the squash plants have the spot to themselves. This planting method gives you two crops from one garden plot. If you have a wire fence, try growing your squash vines over it to save space. The vines are strong enough to hold the hanging fruits.

Bush Winter Squash

Acorn Table King—one lb. (85 days-K); *Burpee's Butterbush*—one lb. (75 days-C); *Gold Nugget* (85 days-I).

Unlike other winter squashes, you can grow these varieties in limited space. Plant in hills three to four feet apart. Thin to three plants per hill.

Spaghetti Squash

Spaghetti Squash (90 days).

When cooked, this squash separates into spaghetti-like strands. The fruits weigh three to five pounds. One hill will provide more than you can handle. Serve the cooked pulp with a traditional tomato pasta sauce or simply with butter. This squash keeps extremely well.

PUMPKINS

Small Sugar or New England Pie—five to seven lbs. (110 days-C,I); *Connecticut Field*—fifteen to twenty lbs.; for the classic Jack O' Lantern (115 days-P,I); *Spirit Hybrid*—fifteen lbs.; semi-bush variety (100 days-C,P).

—HINTS—

Try pumpkin soup. Boil peeled and diced pumpkin, puree by hand or with a food processor, add milk, butter, salt and pepper, a dash of cayenne, and serve over croutons.

Do not throw away pumpkin or squash seeds. Turn them into snack food. Separate the seeds from the stringy innards. Don't wash them. Mix the seeds with some salt and two tablespoons of oil, spread on a cookie sheet, and bake for about one hour at 250 degrees F. Or, you can bake them for fifteen minutes at 375 degrees F.—expect the seeds to pop.

TOMATOES

Some tomatoes grow tall and some grow short. Continuous-growing varieties are called indeterminate, and varieties that stop growing at a certain height, with blossoms at the end of the stems, are called determinate. Indeterminate varieties need staking, while determinate varieties need only limited staking or none at all. Usually seed catalogs tell you what kind of growth to expect from the varieties you select, whether they're determinate or indeterminate. You can plan your tomato patch accordingly.

In cold climates home gardeners judge their tomatoes by their earliness and their flavor. Gardeners are challenged by the desire to pick a ripe tomato by the Fourth of July, never mind the size. But many also live for fattening their egos by showing off the largest tomato they can produce.

To meet these goals, the varieties you grow will determine your success.

If you start your tomatoes from seeds, plant them indoors six weeks before the last expected frost. When transplanting, remove a shovelful of soil for each transplant. Add compost or well-rotted manure and one tablespoon of bone meal, all well mixed with soil. Tomato plants gain vigor if you set them deeply, covering part of the stems, up to the first leaves, with soil.

To encourage the plants to grow extra strong use the trenching method. Make a trench four inches deep, amend the soil, and lay the tomato plant flat in the trench. Bend the tip of the plant upwards and fill the trench with soil, covering the roots and stem up to the first leaves.

If you do not want to bend the plant you can push some soil underneath the upper portion of the plant to form a pillow. Cover the roots and stem with soil. The plant will straighten itself, and the buried stem will rapidly grow new roots.Tomato plants mulched with black plastic grow faster.

PRUNING: Pruning does not always result in larger yields, but it does result in larger tomatoes. Partially pruning tall tomato plants makes sense. At the end of August prune the tips of all stems with flowers or small fruits. These will produce fruits that will never ripen before the first frost, so pruning will strengthen the more mature tomatoes.

Do not prune determinate varieties.

STAKING: Place stakes on the north sides of the tomato plants, preferably at planting time to avoid damaging the roots.

CAGES: You can purchase cages at hardware stores or nurseries. They allow for good circulation of air, thus helping to curb diseases. At the same time, the fruits are kept off the ground and well exposed to the sun.

You can make your own cages out of concrete-reinforcing wire or hog wire, but make sure the mesh is large enough for your hands to reach through and harvest the tomatoes. For indeterminate tomatoes the ideal size for a cage is twenty-four inches in diameter and four feet high. You can vary the size according to the growing pattern of the tomato variety. Secure the cage with stakes or set it three to four inches in the ground.

For determinate varieties, you can fashion a garden fence, eighteen inches high, into a cage. You can purchase garden fencing at nurseries or hardware stores; it has spikes already attached, so all you have to do is set it over the plant. You can vary the diameter of the cage will also vary with the variety of the tomato.

TOMATO TOWERS: You can purchase circular tomato towers made out of wire at nurseries and many hardware stores. They are inexpensive and support strong-stemmed tomato plants fairly well.

Extra Early Tomatoes

Pixie Hybrid (52 days-C); *Northern Light* (55 days-H); *Rocket* (53 days-F); *Gem State*— two-oz. fruits (58 days-I,H); *Glacier* (55 days-F); *Siberian*— three-oz. fruits (59 days-A,H); *Patio Prize Hybrid* (52 days-P); *Edelrot* (55 days-A); *Prairie Fire*—four- to five-oz. fruits (53 days-F).

These determinate varieties reliably produce large numbers of good-tasting fruits. Staking is unnecessary because they grow less than two feet tall. However, the weight of the fruits will bend the stems. A low, wire cage, fifteen to eighteen inches in diameter, gives the best support for this type of plant. Set plants twelve to fifteen inches apart.

Early Tomatoes

Early Girl (54 days-C,G); *Early Cascade* (63 days-J,Q); *Earlibright* (60 days-P,H); *Fireball* (60 days-P); *Manitoba*—six-oz. fruits (60 days-P); *Santiam* (55 days-K,Q); *Oregon Spring*—first fruits are seedless (60 days-K,H,Q); *Starfire*—seven- to eight-oz. fruits (60 days-P,F).

All the early varieties are determinate except for *Early Girl* and *Early Cascade*. These two need staking. As with the extra-early determinate varieties, early determinate varieties grow well in wire cages, but eighteen to twenty inches across for these plants.

Main Season Tomatoes

Fantastic Hybrid (70 days-P,Q); *Bonny Best* (70 days-B,H); *Rutgers*—eight-oz. fruits (75 days-B,C); *Floramerica Hybrid* (75 days-J,M,P); *Nepal*—ten- to twelve-oz. fruits (78 days-I,H); *Better Boy Hybrid* (72 days-C,P); *Celebrity Hybrid*—twelve- to fourteen-oz. fruits (70 days-G,P); *Delicious*—fourteen- to sixteen-oz. fruits (actually fourteen to sixteen oz. is the beginner's size; *Delicious* is the variety for the boastful gardener) (78 days-G,B).

Late Tomatoes

Oxheart—heart-shaped fruits (85 days-B,K); *Climbing*—sixteen-oz. fruits (in a cold climate, it will reach less than its advertised fifteen feet, but trained on a trellis or grown in a cage, it will reward you with beautiful crimson fruits) (90 days-C).

Both varieties produce large, flavorful, meaty fruits with small seed cavities.

Cherry Tomatoes

Gardener's Delight or Sugar Lump—needs staking (68 days-I); *Red Cherry*—needs staking (70 days-G); *Small Fry Hybrid*—needs staking (65 days-J); *Sweet 100* (70 days-C,G); *Whippersnapper*—oval fruits on a ground-hugging plant that grows six to eight inches tall (52 days-I); *Cheerio*—grows two feet tall and needs staking or caging (55 days-I).

Paste or Italian Tomatoes

Nova (65 days-P); *Bellstar* (70 days-I,P); *Heinz 2653* (68 days-I); *Ropreco* (70 days-Q).

All these varieties are determinate and grow about eighteen inches tall; they become bushy and produce three to five ounce oval-shaped fruits. You don't need to stake them, but a wire cage keeps the fruits off the ground. Paste tomatoes produce heavily.

Paste tomatoes have a low juice content, which is good if you are interested in canning. However, they taste good as well; you can use paste tomatoes in fresh salads.

Paste tomatoes have an additional advantage: In cold climates, gardeners often end up with many green tomatoes at the end of the growing season. Because of their low juice content, green paste tomatoes ripen nicely indoors without rotting.

—HINT—

Toast a slice of bread; sprinkle with olive oil. Chop one paste tomato, fresh basil, one clove of garlic; add salt and pepper. Spread the mixture on the bread. You have just prepared a healthy lunch or a gourmet appetizer. For a different version, cut a length of slim, crusty French loaf; butter it, and toast it under the broiler. Then proceed with the rest of the recipe.

Yellow Tomatoes

Gold Nugget—cherry tomato, determinate (60 days-I); *Yellow Pear*—small pear-shaped fruits, determinate (70 days-K); *Yellow Plum*—small plum-shaped fruits, determinate (70 days-M); *Taxi*—baseball-sized fruits, determinate (64 days-I); *Hybrid Lemon Boy*—seven-oz. fruits on tall plant that needs staking, indeterminate (72 days-G,Q).

Winter Storage Tomatoes

Long Keeper—refuses to go bad; it keeps until March, but the taste is below par (78 days-C,Q).

WATERMELONS

Garden Baby Hybrid—short vines with five- to seven-lb. fruits (70 days-I,Q); *Yellow Doll Hybrid*—semicompact vines with five- to six-lb. fruits (65 days-K,Q); *Golden Crown Hybrid*—seven lbs. (75 days-K).

Watermelons, even more than cantaloupes, need warm weather. These icebox-sized varieties are better adapted to cold climates.

Varieties for a Small Garden

Don't feel discouraged by what you feel is inadequate garden space. You can grow a fair amount of vegetables in containers of various sizes. You can even intrude in your flower beds. Limited space is no longer the problem it once was. We can thank the plant breeders for giving us a good selection of vegetables for the small garden or the small appetite. To make things interesting, most of these breeds are early vegetables.

Here are some to consider:

Bush Beans
Two square feet of any bush bean variety will provide you with abundant pods.

Cabbage
Darkri Hybrid—six to eight inch heads (42 days-L); *Earliana*—five-inch wide heads (60 days-C).

Cantaloupe
*Musketee*r (90 days-L); *Bush Star Hybrid* (82 days-C); *Minnesota Midget* (60 days-P).

Carrots
Lady Fingers (62 days-L); *Baby Spike* (52 days-L); *Minicor* (55 days-I).

Cucumbers
(Slicing) *Bush Whopper* (55 days-L); *Salad Bush Hybrid* (57 days-L); *Champion,* (55 days-C); (Pickling) *Bush Pickle* (45 days-L).

Lettuce
Tom Thumb—butterhead (65 days-L); *Minetto*—head lettuce (80 days-C); *Little Gem*—romaine (65 days-C); *Bibb* (60 days).

Peas
(Chinese) *Snowbird* (58 days-C).

Summer Squash
Dixie Hybrid—yellow squash (50 days-L); *Gold Rush* (45 days-L); *Green Magic Hybrid* (48 days-L).

Tomatoes
Pixie Hybrid—two-oz. fruits (52 days-C); *Gem State*—two-oz. fruits (58 days-I); *Stupice*—five-oz. fruits (60 days-A); *Oregon Spring*—six- to seven-oz. fruits (60 days-K); *Whippersnapper*—cherry tomatoes (52 days-I).

Save Your Seeds

THE CLIPPER

You will save plenty of money by growing and saving your own seeds. But you will also accomplish something more important. You will develop varieties truly adapted to your climate, naturally selected to fit your garden's environment.

As your gardening skills develop, so will your preference for certain varieties. As time passes, you will notice that certain varieties grow better for you. This may lead you to want to save the seeds from your favorite plants.

The seeds you buy from large seed companies have been grown where climatic conditions are optimal for the seed variety. For instance, seed companies contract growers to raise tomato or cantaloupe seeds in areas where the plants have time to reach full ripeness. So many seeds listed in seed catalogs have been grown outside of your geographic area. When you plant seeds from another area in your garden, the plants often are less productive. By saving seeds from your most successful plants, you select for the characteristics best suited to your region, thereby adapting the plant to your garden's climate.

However, saving the seeds of any hybrids you've been raising is futile. Some will be sterile, and others will exhibit the traits of only one of the plants cross-bred to produce the parent plant. But, a place for hybrids exists in a garden. They can be especially useful to beginning gardeners, who appreciate their vigor and dependable yields.

A cold climate limits what seeds you can save. You will usually only want to save seeds from annual vegetables, that is, vegetables that bloom and produce seeds in the same year. You will find that saving the seeds of vegetables that bloom in the second year—biennials—is more involved and less practical.

You must consider the propagation behavior of each vegetable when you decide to save seeds. Flowers produce seeds after pollination has occurred, but not all flowers are pollinated in the same way.

Some self-pollinate, and others are cross-pollinated. A flower containing both male and female parts can self-pollinate. On the other hand, a flower that must receive pollen from another flower of the same species is cross-pollinated. Self-pollinated flowers give you seeds true to their type, but you either need to isolate flowers that cross-pollinate, or restrict your garden to one variety of each cross-pollinated vegetable to preserve their purity.

Selecting Plants for Seeds

For cross-pollinated plants, save more than one plant (except for squash—one is enough). Select healthy plants, and stick to one variety from each vegetable. For self-pollinating plants, save just one for seeds. However, if you plant several varieties of peppers, eggplants, or tomatoes—and you want to assure your seeds' purity—you have to keep the plants separate from one another, in spite of the fact that they self-pollinate. Otherwise, they will cross-pollinate, giving unpredictable results. Do not save seeds from diseased plants.

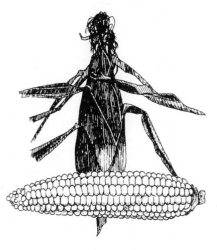

How to Save Seeds

Corn: *Cross-pollinated*

The tassel—the flower above the cob—is the pollen producing male flower, and the silk of the cob is the pollen receiving female flower. Wind blows pollen from one plant to another, ensuring pollination and kernel formation. Pick the ears when the husks have turned brown. Pull the husks, and let the ears hang in a dry place. Loosen the kernels by holding the cob in your hands and twisting.

Cucumbers: *Cross-pollinated*

By the end of the summer a mature cucumbers become yellow. Open a yellow cucumber, and put the seeds in a glass with some of the pulp. Let the seeds and pulp stand for a few days. The mixture will start to ferment, making it easier for you to separate the pulp from the seeds. Keep the seeds that sink to the bottom of the glass, and discard the ones floating on top. Wash the seeds until they are clean, and dry them on paper.

Eggplant: *Self-pollinated*
Cut the fruit and dish out the seeds with some of the pulp. Wash until the seeds separate from the pulp. Dry the seeds on paper.

Leeks: *Cross-pollinated*
Any leek that has wintered over will bloom the following spring, shooting out a long stem with a flower head. When the black seeds start to show, cut the stem and put it head-first in a paper bag. Shake the stem and the seeds will drop out.

Lettuce—Leaf and Butterhead: *Self-pollinated*
You can grow more than one variety and save your seeds. Select a plant that goes to seed late. In other words, save seeds from slow-bolting plant. When the lettuce stalk becomes covered with white fuzz, pull the plant, and hang it upside down with its head stuck in a paper bag. To collect your seeds, simply shake the plant and the seeds will fall to the bottom of the bag. If you let the plant dry with the head unprotected, the seeds will all scatter.
Our summers are too short for crisp head lettuce to bloom and for you to collect seeds.

Muskmelons: *Cross-pollinated*
Collect and wash the seeds and pulp as you would with a cucumber. You'll find it easier to separate melon seeds from the pulp than with a cucumber; only a few washings may do the job.

Peas: *Self-pollinated*
Peas can cross-pollinate, so plant each variety in a different area of your garden. Select the plants from which you want to save seeds, and do not touch them until the pods are dry, but not too dry. You have to pull the plants before the pods shatter, and they shatter easily! Collect the pods and let them dry on a sheet of paper.

Edible-Podded Peas: *Self-pollinated*
These peas belong to a different species than regular peas, and the two species do not cross-pollinate.

Peppers: *Self-pollinated*
Although peppers self-pollinate, separate your sweet peppers from the hot ones. They have been known to cross-pollinate. In addition, give each variety its own patch. A pepper is ripe when it turns red, either on the plant or after picking. Peppers have by far the easiest seeds to collect. Open the fruit, separate the seeds and let them dry.

Radishes: *Cross-pollinated*
Select a few plants that have healthy roots, and thin to one foot apart. You will find that a radish plant starts small, but by the time you collect the seeds you have a bush on your hands. The mature seed pods are small and brown. Either open the pods by hand or run a rolling pin over them to encourage shattering. One plant gives enough seeds for you and your neighbors!

Spinach: *Cross-pollinated*
Spinach is a frustrating plant from which to save seeds. First of all, collect seeds from slow-bolting plants—and in our climate, most spinach plants bolt early. To complicate things, spinach has separate male and female plants. (The male plants are smaller and should be pulled out because they give poor quality seeds. This selective removal is called "rogueing.") When the stalks on the remaining plants turn brown, pull the plants and dry them in the sun. You can loosen the seeds by rubbing the plant with your hands.

Squash, Pumpkin: *Cross-pollinated*
Squash cross-pollination is a controversial subject among gardeners. We hear many funny tales about strangely-formed squash growing from seeds saved by gardeners. One reason for this could be cross-pollination. Botonists divide squash into four species. Varieties of any one species will cross-pollinate, but no cross-pollination occurs between species. For instance, zucchini will not cross with hubbard squash, which belongs to a different species. Gardeners usually don't know what species of squash they have planted, partially because most seed catalogs don't provide this information.

Leave summer squash to mature until the fruit hardens. Winter squash hardens as it ripens. To collect the seeds, cut the fruits, pick out the seeds with your hands, then wash and dry them.

Tomatoes: *Self-pollinated*

You can grow more than one variety in your garden. If you want total purity, plant each variety in a different spot; bees might cause some crossing. Be sure the tomatoes you select for seeds are not diseased. (A cracked fruit is not diseased. It has broken open because of inconsistent watering.) Cut the tomatoes and place the seeds in a fine sieve, run water through it until the seeds are clean, and let them dry on some paper. You can, if you wish, place the pulp and seeds in a glass with some water for a few days and let fermentation separate them. The good seeds will drop to the bottom of the glass. Remove and dry them.

Care of Your Seeds

Some of your seeds might need cleaning. You can separate chaff, leaves, and other light materials from the seeds by winnowing. To do this, you need a windy day. Standing outside, with a breeze blowing, drop the seeds into a bucket, and the wind will blow away the light material. Repeat until the seeds are clean.

Store your seeds in a cool, dark, and dry place. Place your seeds in covered glass jars to help them retain moisture. Or, if you prefer an easier method, put your seeds in labeled envelopes.

To test your seeds' viability when you're ready to plant, place a few between two layers of paper towels, and put the towels in a saucer. Moisten the towels and insert the saucer in a plastic bag. Don't tie it; just fold it under the saucer. Put the saucer in a warm place, and check for germination in three to four days, keeping in mind that some seeds will take longer than others.

CHAPTER 7

Herbs In Your Garden

Varieties for Your Garden

Your garden is incomplete without herbs. Once you use fresh herbs in your kitchen, you'll always make them a part of your garden. Herbs are also a blessing if you are on a restricted sodium diet; they enhance your food's flavor without being detrimental to your health.

You should grow perennial herbs in a place where you can leave them, since they require permanent beds. You can place annual herbs wherever you find a spot, or even along the edges of your garden. Many herbs will protect other plants from a variety of pests. (See *Companion Planting*, page 65.)

The following herbs can be grown in any cold-climate garden:

Basil: *Annual, one foot tall.*
This herb is indispensable for Italian sauces. It is the basic ingredient for pesto, a paste added to soups or pasta. For best results, start it indoors and transplant seedlings twelve inches apart.

Borage: *Annual, two to three feet tall.*
The young leaves of this plant taste like cucumber, and can be added to salads. When older, the leaves become covered with fuzz, making them difficult to use. The plant has attractive, star-like, edible blue flowers that draw bees to your garden. You can plant borage directly outdoors. It reseeds itself, and one plant provides sufficient greens and blooms for most gardeners.

Catnip: *Perennial, two to three feet tall, bushy.*
Catnip has two uses: Your cat will love playing with it, and you will enjoy the refreshing cold or warm tea brewed from its leaves. Catnip flowers attract bees. You can plant it directly outdoors. It reseeds itself and will also return the following year. Plant a few catnip plants around your cabbage patch to deter white butterflies.

Camomile, German: *Hardy annual, one to two feet tall.*
Camomile has tiny, daisy-like flowers used to make tea. You can plant it directly in your garden, and it blends nicely with other flowers. It blooms continuously all summer. When you use the blooms for tea, use only five to six flowers per cup or the flavor becomes overpowering.

Chervil: *Hardy annual, one foot tall.*
This plant's feathery leaves look similar to parsley, but they have a licorice flavor. Use the leaves in fish and egg dishes. You can seed it directly outdoors.

Chives: *Perennial, one foot tall.*
This popular herb has an onion flavor. It takes little room and provides cuttings throughout the summer. It forms attractive, light-purple flowers; cut them off for a longer yield of chives. You can grow it from seeds or propagate it by dividing an established clump. Plant one to two divisions. Plant your chives among your roses—chives deter aphids.

Coriander, Cilantro, or Chinese Parsley: *Annual, two to three feet tall.*
Plant coriander directly in your garden because it dislikes being transplanted. Use coriander in soups and special dishes. Its strong flavor takes getting used to. Thin seedlings to four to five inches apart.

Dill: *Annual, two to three feet tall.*
Dill leaves make excellent additions to salads and many other dishes; use the seeds and stems in pickling. Plant directly outside. Thin to one foot apart. Do not panic if you see aphids on your dill plants. Dill attracts aphids, and seeing aphids on the plants does not necessarily mean your garden has become infested.

Lovage: *Perennial, two to three feet tall.*
The leaves of this plant make a good substitute for celery. It grows vigorously even in a cold climate. You can use the seeds in breads or meat loaf. Two plants provide enough leaves and seeds for a family. You can start lovage from seed or propagate it from a root division.

Marjoram: *Annual, one foot tall.*
This low-growing herb has many uses and is a must in any garden. Start the seeds indoors, and transplant the seedlings ten inches apart. When harvesting, leave about one inch of stems on the plant for continuous regrowth.

Oregano: *Perennial, one foot tall.*
Unfortunately, it is difficult to locate true oregano seeds. Too often what seed companies sell as oregano turns out to be marjoram. Keep experimenting with seed companies until you get the real thing. Oregano leaves are smoother and larger than marjoram leaves.
To make matters more confusing, herb growers disagree over what is true oregano. Some gardeners say the *Oreganum vulgare*, which grows two feet tall with purplish flowers, is true oregano. Others say the less hardy Greek variety, *Oreganum heraclesticum*, which grows less tall and has white flowers, is true oregano. No matter where you stand on the

question, this herb tastes outstanding, and is an indispensable ingredient in spaghetti sauce.

True oregano winters-over poorly.

Plant one foot apart. When you harvest oregano, cut the stems one inch above the roots to allow the plant to regrow.

Sage: *Perennial, one to two feet tall, bushy.*
You can start the seeds indoors, but germination is difficult. You will find it easier to grow sage if you buy the plant from a nursery. One plant provides more than enough leaves to season your meats and dressings.

Spearmint: *Perennial, one to two feet tall.*
Use the leaves in cooking and for teas. Start from seeds or cuttings. Once you establish spearmint in your garden you need to periodically check its growth; it spreads easily. Instead of starting from seed, you can use cuttings from someone who wants to control their patch.

Summer Savory: *Annual, one foot tall.*
You can use this herb in practically every dish. It makes the best herbal substitute for salt. Start seeds indoors for best results. Space seedlings eight inches apart when you transplant. Plant generously. Cut and dry your savory when the flowers begin to appear.

Thyme: *Perennial, one foot tall, bushy.*
Use the leaves to season meats, stews and sauces. Start seeds indoors. Thyme grows with little care and looks decorative enough to use as a border. Two plants provide adequate numbers of leaves for most gardeners.

Tarragon (French): *Perennial, two feet tall, bush type.*
When you order tarragon, you have to be specific—ask for French. Russian tarragon grows well, but has a disappointing flavor. Avoid buying any tarragon that's not specifically labeled as French. You can use this miracle herb in salads, with chicken, in egg dishes, in sauces, and in vinegars. In the spring, when tarragon shoots are tender, add the leaves and stems to your dishes. Try some tarragon with your fried rice for a new taste experience. Later in the season you can dry tarragon for winter use. Tarragon propagates by cuttings, and one plant will provide enough leaves for most gardeners. It spreads by sending out underground runners.

Preserving Your Herbs

Collect your herbs just before the flowers fully open. Gather herbs in the morning after the dew dries and before the heat sets in. At this time the oils and flavors reach their peak. Wash the herbs only if they are dusty. Wash in cold water, shake, and pat dry with paper towels. Then gather the herbs into small bundles, tie with a string, and hang in an airy, dark place. If you don't have a dark place to hang your herbs, put a paper bag over the bundles, securing it around the stems with a rubber band. This also protects the bundles from dust. Do not dry herbs in full sun because they will lose their color and fragrance. After approximately two weeks the herbs dry to the point where they crumble easily. Strip the leaves from the stems.

You can also dry herb leaves you have removed from the stems. Spread them on a newspaper and let them dry. The quickest way to dry herbs is in a microwave. Place the herbs between two paper towels, and microwave them for one minute. This technique works well for basil and parsley, which tend to darken when air dried. Of course, you can also use a conventional oven. Place the herbs on a split-open brown paper bag. Place in a 150-degree F. oven for a few hours, with the oven door ajar. Keep checking your herbs as they dry.

Dried herbs store well in glass jars. Keep them in a dark place to preserve their color.

You can freeze herbs after chopping them. Place them in plastic bags and take out the desired amount without thawing. This method works well when preserving herbs for a short time. For long-term storage, freeze chopped herbs with some water in ice cube trays. Once frozen, store the cubes in plastic bags in the freezer. When a recipe calls for an herb, simply pop out an ice cube, and add it to the broth.

Some herbs grow well indoors in pots. Put them on your kitchen window sill and they will provide fresh herbs during the snowy months. Thyme, chives, and basil are most cooks' favorites.

Epilogue

Gardening and Therapy

Through the efforts you put into planning and tending a garden you can reap many non-material rewards. Yes, plants demand attention, but they don't talk back, they don't order you around, and they don't disrupt your life by telephoning. They represent a world opposite to that "jungle out there." To be sure, with your loving care, your garden might come to resemble a lush jungle itself. But it won't land you on the psychiatrist's couch!

APPENDIX I

Seed Companies

The following list is by no means complete. However, these companies are all reliable, and the novice gardener can confidently order from them. You can purchase many of the varieties recommended in this book at supermarkets and gardening stores. Some of the brands to look for are Northrup King, Lilly Miller, Excel, Burpee, and Ferry-Morse.

INDEPENDENT SEED COMPANIES
SENSITIVE TO REGIONAL NEEDS

Abundant Life Seed Foundation
P.O. Box 772
Port Townsend, WA 98368

Organic and untreated seeds,
heirloom vegetables.

Bountiful Gardens
19550 Walker Road
Willits, CA 95490

Over 230 untreated, open-
pollinated seeds.

Seeds Blum
Idaho City Stage
Boise, ID 83706

Heirloom seeds and hard
to find varieties.

Clark Seed Company
Drawer D
Kenton, DE 19955

Serving regional needs.

Comstock Ferre & Company
263 Main Street
Wethersfeld, CT 06109

Serving regional needs with old
and new varieties.

The Cook's Garden
P.O. Box 65
Londonderry, VT 05148

Specializes in good-tasting
varieties; a large selection of
lettuce and greens.

Fisher's Garden Store
P.O. Box 236
Belgrade, MT 59714

Varieties for short seasons;
breed varieties for cold climates.

Fox Hollow Herbs
P.O. Box 148
McGrann, PA 16236

Herbs, vegetables, and flowers;
devoted to cutting gardening
costs with "$.35 Seed Samplers."

Garden City Seeds
1324 Crow Road
Victor, MT 59875

Specializes in open-pollinated
and organically grown seeds for
cold climates.

High Altitude Gardens
P.O. Box 4619
Ketchum, ID 83340

Varieties selected for high
altitudes and cold climates. A
large selection of tomato
varieties, imported directly
from Russia.

Nichols Garden Nursery
1190 North Pacific Highway.
Albany, OR 97321

Dependable and unusual
varieties, good herbs.

Shepherd's Garden Seeds
30 Irene Street
Torrington, CT 06790

Specializes in European
varieties.

Southern Exposure Seed
Exchange
P.O. Box 158
North Garden, VA 22959

Open-pollinated, heirloom,
traditional varieties listed in an
informative catalog.

Territorial
P.O. Box 157
Cottage Grove, OR

Specializes in early and flavorful
varieties.

LARGE SEED COMPANIES

W. Atlee Burpee & Co.
300 Park Avenue
Warminster, PA 18991-0001

De Giorgi Seed Company
1529 North Saddle Creek Road
Omaha, NE 68104

Farmer Seed & Nursery
818 N.W. Fourth Street
Faribault, MN 55021

Gurney Seed & Nursery
Page Street
Yankton, SD 57079

Harris Seed
60 Saginaw Drive
Rochester, NY 14623

Henry Field Seed & Nursery Co.
P.O. Box 700, Dept. 87-5997
Oak Street
Shenandoah, IA 51602

Johnny's Selected Seeds
Foss Hill Road
Albion, ME 14910

J.W. Jung Co.
Randolph, WI 53956

Park Seed
Cokesbury Road
Greenwood, SC 29647-0001

Rocky Mountain Seed Co.
P.O. Box 5204
Denver, CO 80217-5204

R.H. Shumway, Seedsman
P.O. Box 777
Rockford, IL 61105

Stokes Seeds, Inc.
P.O. Box 548
Buffalo, NY 14240

Otis S. Twilly Seed Co.
P.O. Box 65
Trevose, PA 19047

CANADIAN SEED COMPANIES

William Dam Seeds, Ltd.
P.O. Box 8400
Dundas, Ontario
Canada L9H 6M1
Untreated vegetable seeds, European varieties.

Dominion Seed House and
Country Garden Center
Highway 7 & Maple Avenue
Georgetown, Ontario
Canada L7G 4A2
Large mail order catalog.

Siberia Seeds
Box 2528
Olds, Alberta
Canada T0M 1P0
Heirloom and cold climate tomato varieties.

Stokes Seeds
Box 10
St. Catherines, Ontario
Canada L2R 6R6
Large selection for the home gardener and grower.

Territorial Seed Co.
P.O. Box 46225
Station G
3760 West Tenth Avenue
Vancouver, B.C.
Canada V6R 4G5
Varieties for gardeners west of
the Cascades.

Vesey's Seeds Limited
York, Prince Edward Island
Canada C0A 1P0
Specializes in short season
varieties.

Stanley Zubrowski
Box 26
Prairie River, Saskatchewan
Canada S0E 1J0
Good selection of tomato
varieties.

SPECIALIZED SEED COMPANIES

Herb Society of America Inc.
9019 Kirtland-Chardon Road
Mentor, OH 44060
Good source of information on
herbs.

Le Jardin du Gourmet
P.O. Box 75
St. Johnsbury Center, VT 05863
Shallots, leeks, garlic, herbs, and
French varieties.

Kitazawa Seed Co.
1748 Laine Avenue
Santa Clara, CA 95051-3012
Japanese vegetable seeds.

The Pepper Gal
10536 119th Avenue
Largo, FL 34643
200 pepper varieties.

Richters
Box 26
Goodwood, Ontario
Canada L0C 1A0
Wide selection of herbs.

Ronniger's Seed Potatoes
Star Route Moyie Springs
Moyie Springs, ID 83845
Seed potatoes.

Sunrise Enterprises
P.O. Box 10058
Elmwood, CT 06110-0058
Large selection of Oriental
vegetables.

Tomato Growers Supply Co.
P.O. Box 2237
Fort Myers, FL 33902
Wide selection of tomato and
pepper varieties.

SOURCES FOR HEIRLOOM VARIETIES

After closely reading seed catalogs for a few years, you will notice that varieties appear and disappear without explanation—especially hybrid varieties. This phenomenon becomes even more pronounced when a large corporation buys out a seed company.

Gardeners can counteract this fickle market by saving seeds from their open-pollinated varieties and swapping with other gardeners. And, if you can no longer find a particular variety in the catalogs, check one of the following sources that specialize in traditional varieties and their preservation.

Graham Center Seed and Nursery Directory
Rural Advancement Fund
P.O. Box 1029
Pittsboro, NC 27312

The directory lists the sources for open-pollinated variety seed companies where available. Write for the directory and its cost.

Seed Savers Exchange
R.R. 3, Box 239
Decorah, IA 52101

Kent Whealy is the director. A $25 membership includes the Winter Yearbook, the Summer Edition, and the Fall Harvest Edition. Also available, but not included in the membership, is an inventory of seed catalogs listing all open-pollinated varieties that you can find in the United States and Canada.

Useful Literature

PERIODICALS

Harrowsmith Magazine
Queen Victoria Road
Camden East, Ontario
Canada K0K 1J0

The Herb Quarterly
P.O. Box 548
Boiling Springs, PA 17007

National Gardening
P.O. Box 52874
Boulder, CO 80322-2874

Organic Gardening
33 East Minor Street
Emmaus, PA 18049

BOOKS

Bagg, Alma W. *Cooking Without a Grain of Salt.* Bantam Books.

Country Wisdom Bulletins. Storey Publishing, Dep't. 9001, Schoolhouse
Road, VT 05260 (or call toll-free 800-441-5700):
Attracting Birds
Build Your Own Underground Root Cellar
Building and Using Cold Frames
Improving Your Soil
Grow Super Salad Greens
'SCAT' Pest-Proofing Your Garden
What Every Gardener Should Know About Earthworms
Wide-row Planting

Jeavons, John. *How to Grow More Vegetables (than you ever thought possible on less land than you can imagine).* Ten Speed Press, 159 pp. (Devoted to intensive gardening.)

Morash, Marian. *The Victory Garden Cookbook.* Alfred A. Knopf, 374 pp. (A gardening and cookbook combined. Worth every penny!)

Rodale, Robert, ed. *The Basic Book of Organic Gardening.* Ballantine Books, 361 pp. (Basic and informative.)

U.S. Department of Agriculture. *Storing Vegetables and Fruits in Basement, Cellars, Outbuildings, and Pits.* Home and Garden Bulletin No. 119. Government Printing Office. Washington, D.C. 20402. (Or order from the Consumer Information Center, Pueblo, CO 81009.)

Index